Latin Loving: Secrets of a Latin Woman to Capture a Man's Heart

Betty Heisler

ISBN-13: 9780970307835
ISBN-10: 0970307837

To my daughter Iliana, the constant love of my life,
and to lovers everywhere. May true love find you.

I have loved well and deep,
and not too often.
But I have loved.
And that, my friend
has served me well.
For I have given
of myself
without reserve
and in so doing
have taken flight
time and again.
For I have loved,
And I have done it well.

Books by Betty Heisler

The Last Minyan in Havana

Under the Shade of the Ceiba Tree

Meet Me in Hong Kong

Contents

Prologue

I arrived in Miami with a suitcase full of hand-sewn dresses and little else. Once it was decided that I was to leave Cuba, it would have been unheard of for me to embark on such a fateful trip without a proper wardrobe.

Little did I know then that not quite a year later, the place where I took my first tentative steps into the realm of the written word would be brutally pulverized by a counter revolutionary bomb. The eyesore that bomb left--an empty city block in the middle of downtown Havana-- would later be turned by Castro's government into a badly-kept park, a revolutionary reminder of the former shrine to capital consumerism that El Encanto, the elegant department store where I used to intern as an advertising copy writer, once was.

But that blissful afternoon in Miami Beach, Sherry, my American cousin, and I were just two teenagers excitedly poring over the contents of my suitcase and chatting about the latest fashions as we went through the dresses that Magda, my mother's Cuban dressmaker had whipped up for me on such a short notice.

I was particularly fond of a mauve Italian cotton dress that had come out of the pages of French Vogue. With a U-shaped neckline and draped in the front, it was the image of European sophistication. Imagine my surprise the following week when, having been invited to my first mixer at the home of one of my cousin's friends, the only girl in a dress was me. All the American girls wore straight skirts and tops accessorized by either trendy ballerina shoes or loafers. I felt like someone from another planet with my skin tight, scooped-necked number and my four-inch stilettos trying to converse in my halting English with the boys that surrounded me like bees hovering over a transplanted strange exotic flower. Well, I did stand out...

I ended up dating one of those boys for about a month until Charles, my Cuban high school sweetheart followed me to Miami. We were married shortly after, and within four years had started a family. During that time I tried to learn everything I could about my new country while I raised two small children, and eventually was able to continue my education, which had been interrupted when I left Havana. This time I pursued a journalism degree, and upon graduation started to work for the Spanish editions of Harper's Bazaar and Cosmopolitan, eventually becoming an editor of a teen magazine, with the same publishing group.

Just turning thirty six, and my children ten and fourteen, my husband died suddenly of a mysterious illness. Fortunately I had my career, but loneliness overwhelmed me whenever the clock would strike six and no one would come through the door. I was alone with no single friends, since at my age all of my friends were married.

In time a neighbor introduced me to a girlfriend who was also single. But I had no clue as to how to behave as a single woman, having been married at the age of twenty. The rules had definitely changed, and I felt like an uninvited guest at a housewarming party.

I read every relationship book I could get my hands on, but I was coming from a different place, a place where men take the initiative when approaching a woman and still open doors for their ladies. I was a Latin woman with the mores and customs of a single woman of Spanish extraction trying to relate to American men in the liberated 80's in Miami. No wonder I was having problems!

I did my share of dating but something always seemed to go wrong. The men I was dating simply were on a different wavelength, one I didn't know how to reach. Finally, I started to take stock of what made me different and learned how to turn those differences to my advantage. Living in the cultural melting pot that others call Miami and I call home, I also started to tune in as a journalist and a writer into the distinctly sensual and subtle ways in which Latin women, whether from Buenos Aires, Havana or Caracas attract their men--with emphasis on the word *attract* (more about that later.)

Being that we all could use some help spicing up our love life while we navigate the treacherous waters of the attraction between the sexes, I would like to share this precious knowledge. I invite you to explore with me, Love, Latin style.

Introduction

Vive la difference!

*M*en and women are different...We think differently, our priorities are different and we view the world in different ways. Thank God for that!

This is a basic fact that in the midst of our quest for equality has been lost in the shuffle. Let's stop for a minute to say that our well-deserved and hard-won equality is here to stay: in the workforce, under the law, I'm all for it. We deserve equal pay for equal work and we should all be the same under the Constitution. But this book is about something else.

This book is about the subtle idiosyncrasies that brand us as women and make men men. Here we are going to talk about the other differences. The ones that made the French declare "Vive la difference!" Long live the difference! The ones that make us act like girls and make men rejoice in the fact that we do. The very important differences that Latin women have never forgotten and that make them irresistible to men.

As a Latin woman, albeit a thoroughly Americanized one, I believe it is high time we share our secret with our American sisters. After all, we're all in this together, aren't we? So grab a cup of strong Cuban coffee, or a glass or Chilean wine, sit in a comfy chair and listen up. Let's start with the basics.

It Takes Two To Tango

What goes on between a man and a woman when they find themselves attracted to each other is like a well-choreographed dance. One takes a step forward, the other one follows with a step backwards. Sort of like *Dancing with the Stars* without the rhinestones. He leads, she follows gracefully. She sways, he catches her. Come to think of it, perhaps the popularity of the show at this point in time may have something to do with our longing for romance and plain sensuality in a world of speed dating and Internet hookups. Look at the costumes: there's enough cleavage and fluttering chiffon to make a Southern belle swoon. And how about the popularity of the tango? Both dancers are locked in an embrace and there's no question as to who's leading.

My friend Ella, who is a tango aficionado, tells me that her weekly tango class is like an hour-long embrace without emotional consequences. Think about it. You are in a man's arms feeling the contours, warmth and firmness of another's body and moving to the cadence of a beautiful song. What could be better? Tango has also been described as "better than sex, because it lasts longer." Well, that point is debatable…

In Argentine tango people dance in close embrace, and if a woman is well endowed, her breasts will end up right against the man's chest. Trust me, this is not a dance for the shy and definitely not for the faint of heart. When you get up to dance tango you'd better like your partner, for you are going to end up becoming intimately familiar with his body. The man leads, putting forth a great deal of macho energy. In the dance world macho has a good connotation, for dancing becomes a distillation of the gender roles through the ages. The male and female energies are raw and exposed, so forget political correctness here and just dance.

Years ago I went dancing with a new beau and I kept getting closer while he kept pushing me away. He wanted to hold me at arm's length, and I felt terribly rejected. It turned out that was the way he had learned to dance, with his right hand extended, so he could concentrate on the steps (he wasn't a very good dancer.) We almost broke up that very evening and I must say we never danced again. So men, believe me, it's OK to hold a woman close while you dance—we like it!

Once I tried to teach a friend to dance bolero, which is slow dancing to Latin music, but he kept focusing on the steps… and bumping into my toes. Finally, I had an inspiration. (I really liked him, so this part was easy. I wouldn't recommend doing this with someone you don't care about and are just teaching how to dance.) I stopped, looked him in the eye and said: "Forget the dancing, just take me in your arms as if you were going to kiss me." That he understood and he took me eagerly in his arms. "Now," I said, "you can start moving with the music." Never had a problem dancing with him again!

Some women find it hard to surrender to being led. These are women who have been indoctrinated into the belief that in order to succeed in the world they have to be assertive and take the first step. When dancing tango you have to do the opposite—you start by taking a step backwards to allow the man to step in and lead you. The roles are very well defined; the man leads, the woman waits and receives—his lead, his step, his energy. What a beautiful metaphor for the role of the sexes! No wonder in these confusing times tango has had such a revival. There are tango groups all over the world and Ella tells me that she feels right at home wherever she goes. Whether in New York, Tokyo or Paris, she finds a tango class to fit right in. By the way, the Japanese are some of the best tango dancers, which is no surprise, for even though they rarely invent anything, whatever the Japanese take on, they often do better than anyone.

But forget about Japan and let's talk about what we have here at home. If you are interested in learning how to dance tango, you don't have to go too far, for there are tango classes everywhere. A couple of years ago I went to a tango class at the Ritz Carlton in Coconut Grove, at the South end of Miami. When I arrived the group of twenty seemed evenly split between men and women, all beautifully dressed. Particularly the women, who dress for the part: lots of chiffon, and the shoes! Oh, the shoes! Tango dancers spend fortunes on dancing shoes. Just as you must feel good in your own skin before being able to interact successfully with the right man, good tango shoes not only have to look good but also must be comfortable enough to allow the wearer to do all those intricate steps. They have to have heels, the higher the better they look, and many have ornaments that make them look really sexy.

As in the relationship between a man and a woman, this is a complex kind of dance with actual choreography and a repertoire of possible moves—walk, cross, pivot. While dancing tango you have to be constantly on alert, for each step is unpredictable because it is improvised by the leader. When he "indicates", the follower (you) must move first, opening the door by extending your leg back. So in essence you are always anticipating what your partner is about to do and then responding. As long as you keep doing that, you can keep dancing... sort of like real life, isn't it?

So yes, it takes two to tango, but each dancer must be keenly aware of the role they play—in life as well as in the dance floor. Being observant is a good trait when you first meet a man. Just as in dancing the tango, observe his moves, get a feel for what makes him tick and learn how to respond. Don't be shy to throw in a bit of your own fancy footwork, but make sure that it's in sync with his own...Learn how to dance to beautiful music together. And above all, in dancing, as well as in life, make sure you don't step on his toes!

1

Ladylike is Sensual

That old adage: be a chef in the kitchen, a mistress in the bedroom and a lady in the drawing room couldn't be truer. The problem is that many women get it completely wrong. They dress like you know what; they fake orgasms and then make reservations for dinner. Now, do you blame a man who looks for the door after a few dates?

Now let's analyze this for a minute. This is what I believe: there is a way to look, and act ladylike and still appear sexy. And I also firmly believe that if the only thing you remember after reading this book is what I'm about to tell you, you are already on your way to score much higher with the next man that comes into your life. Guaranteed. The formula is quite simple. And it has as much to do with your attitude as with the way you present yourself to the world. I'm going to walk you through it, step by step.

Be Sensual, not Only Sexual

In the American culture sensuality is usually equated with sex. That couldn't be farther from the truth! Sensuality has to do with anything we perceive through our senses: things that we hear, touch, see, smell and taste. Somehow we threw in a short circuit long ago and dumped it all into sexiness. And herein lays the allure of the Latin woman. When she spots a man she's interested in, her approach is always soft, not obvious or target-oriented. And in the process beguiling, seductive and mysterious. Sort of like the difference between slow dancing and rock'n'roll.

I truly believe that being sensual is key to how us Latins see—and enjoy—the world. And this is something that is available to all, if we just tune in. I'll give you a few of my favorite sensory delight:

Listening to the fluid, soft melodies of Claire de Lune by Debussy, or your favorite symphony. Have you ever noticed the enraptured faces of the audience at a concert hall? They are being transported into ecstasy by their sense of hearing. A powerful sensual experience!

The feel of the softest silk against my bare skin, or the touch of a baby's cheek against mine.

The ocean air playing with my hair, my face and every part of my body while I walk by the seashore.

Getting into a freshly-made bed with clean, pressed sheets after a long day's work.

The aroma of fresh-roasted coffee first thing in the morning.

An ice-cold glass of lemonade in the heat of a summer afternoon.

Biting into a ripe cold peach in July, the sweet juice filling my parched mouth.

Plunging into the cool, emerald waters of a Caribbean beach early in the morning.

The scent of fresh cut flowers, or your favorite fragrance out of a bottle.

An hour of reflexology, where every toe and square inch of my grateful foot is pummeled and massaged to perfection.

And the ultimate sensual treat. The luscious, velvety texture of a dark chocolate truffle slowly melting over my tongue while the flavor explodes on my taste buds.

You probably have enjoyed some of those pleasures, or perhaps all, but never paid much attention, because you never knew how important they were for your own sensual nature. But that is going to change. Starting today you are going to start putting together your own menu of sensual pleasures. I just shared some of mine with you. Now go ahead and start your own.

You may prefer to listen to a Broadway score instead of Debussy, or your bliss may be to look at the nuances of a Boticello painting instead of the colors of the sky in the Pacific Northwest. You may salivate over Haagen Dazs *dulce de leche* ice cream instead of a chocolate truffle. But whatever sends you, go for it and be present, engage all your senses while you're doing it.

Enjoy the experience thoroughly, become a sensual gourmet and start developing your own sensory muscles. If you do it right, your enhanced sense of enjoyment will help to start drawing men to you like bees go to honey. After all, when all is said and done, and philosophers have pondered this over the centuries, I believe that the real purpose of life is to enjoy. I don't think God would have put us on such a beautiful planet for any other reason!

So go ahead and partake of every delight available to you and see what happens. Remember, everybody loves a lover. You are about to become a lover of life—and men, being the sensual creatures that they are, will begin to follow your trail, if for no other reason, to find out what makes you tick. Your only problem will be to pick the right one. But take your time and explore your options. I promise you will be having so much fun in the process that you won't mind the waiting!

Your Aura

Everyone has an aura that others perceive when they first lay eyes on you. The good news is: that first impression is incredibly long lasting. The bad news is that it is.

When you walk into a room you will bring together a product: you. And it better be well packaged. I'm referring to subtle things that at first may be imperceptible, but work together to create a favorable or negative image. It has to do with the way you put yourself together: your clothes, your makeup, your accessories, and lastly the way you move.

Some women dress for men, some women dress for other women, and at times we may dress one way or the other, depending on the circumstances. Since this book deals with our effect on men, I am going to skip the luncheon dressing and concentrate on the way we dress to capture a man's heart.

Let's start by saying that you should always act —and dress like a lady. I can't say this often enough. Perhaps because my mother instilled it in me since I was a teenager, I have never forgotten it. It always keeps you grounded, and your identity in check. You are, first and foremost, a lady.

But enough of that. Let's get to the juicy part. Let's say that after two weeks of soulful telephone conversations you are finally going to meet the new man you were introduced to by one of your married friends. Can I tell you a secret? Men love women in skirts. So, if you have good legs —and I hope you do, go for it. Wear a skirt. Now beware of the length. Unless you are still in your thirties and are very slim, don't go over two inches above the knee. That will show all of your leg and just the beginning of the thighs without riding up when you sit down, which can be not only déclassé, but also just plain uncomfortable. You don't want to spend the evening adjusting your skirt instead of listening to what he has to say. If I may add, I find when wearing a skirt or a dress, that the easiest ones to wear are knits, since they adjust to your body and most importantly—they stretch...bless their hearts!

If your legs are not your best attribute, or you are carrying a few extra pounds, a good choice would be to wear pants. The good part about pants is that you can wear the highest platform shoes you can find and they will make you look taller and slimmer without him having a clue, since they will be hidden by the pants, giving you a flattering long-legged look he will love.

This is the time to invest in a great top with a V neck to further emphasize the vertical illusion, and accessorize with long chains. Remember, anything vertical will tend to slim you down. The same goes for stripes. Never wear horizontal ones, unless you are Kate Moss's twin sister.

Your Hair

Stay as close as possible to your natural color. That is what nature gave you for your skin tone and it is what defines you. You are either a ravishing brunette, a willowy blonde or a sassy redhead, and all the shades in between. Why fool around with that? You may want to try a lighter shade. As time goes on definitely add a few highlights, but steer clear of radical changes: bleached blonde and raven black are out after forty, and I should add they are never flattering unless you have perfect, very young skin. Not to mention the damage that these extreme processes cause to your hair. Dry and coarse is never pretty. Soft and subtle is what you're aiming for.

Keep your hair healthy and spray-free. Spend more on conditioners and treatments than in styling. Pay top dollar for a good hair cut and color. Better yet, color it yourself. Today's products make it almost fool-proof to enhance your natural shade. Remember, that's all you are going to do—enhance. By staying close to your natural color you are bound to minimize the damage that all hair colors eventually do to the hair shaft. And condition, condition, condition. If you have a good cut and your hair is healthy, you will be able to style it yourself. Keep it simple. If your hair is wavy, go for a wild curly look. If it's straight, just blow dry and set it on rollers. Blow hot hair over the rollers and allow to set for ten minutes, brush and let it fall free. He will love to run his fingers through your hair. Remember, the silkier it feels, the better.

Latin women know that long hair is sexy—at any age. Yes, even after forty! There is nothing more sensual for a man than to run his fingers through your hair. But it has to be touchable, soft hair. Not hair that has been teased and lacquered within one degree of its existence. We know the importance of conditioning and grooming our hair, and some of us still live by the old standby: olive oil inside (in salads and for light stir frying) and outside, a dab on our fingertips after washing our hair. If you still doubt its efficacy, look at the glorious manes of Jennifer Lopez and Penelope Cruz. Yes, they have the best hair dressers, but they also sport thick, bouncy tresses. Leave the pixie haircuts to the likes of Miranda/Cynthia Nixon, Latin women like to bounce our hair as we walk. I just love the feel of it down my back—and think of the possibilities when you're flirting!

You can try the new glazes for added shine and always spray a light coat of perfume pointing at your head. You'll drive him crazy! No matter what you do, take care of your hair. It is like a frame on a beautiful picture: your face. I'm going to leave this topic by sharing this with you: I once had a man tell me that whenever he met a woman, the first thing he fantasized about was seeing her hair spread out on his pillow. Need I say more?

Your Skin

I could write a whole chapter just on touching, but you want to get your knowledge fast, not get a PhD. So let's start with your skin.

Way before dermatologists started warning about the ill effects of sun exposure, us Latin girls were told by our mothers to be careful. After all, we grew up in sunnier climates and we knew that too much of a good thing can be deadly. You will rarely see a Latin woman tanned and wrinkled like a prune. We probably spend more on lotions and treatments than any segment of the population and consider it well worth it. Let's face it girls, we are vain!

Living in Miami I see too many women abusing the sun, and far too many older women with leather-like skin after a few years of living here. Anyway, it's their call, although thank God younger generations are way more careful. Just remember, the soft, caressable parts of you are what ultimately drive him crazy! So keep them that way.

Lucky for us, there never has been a better time to be female and look good. From laser to injectables, to a zillion lotions and creams, it is all there for you. But a word of caution—whatever you decide to do, if it's a cosmetic procedure, doing less is always better than overdoing. You want to look natural, not done. And if you decide to go for a face lift, do it earlier rather than later. This way the doctor will have less skin to lift and the change will be less drastic. You will end up looking refreshed, as if you're coming back from a vacation--instead of an operating room.

A Word About Your Neckline and Other Sexy Garments

I know. Men love women's breasts. And many women are tempted to show them off. That's fine. But don't overdo it. A lady that is well endowed or even one who is less fortunate will let men have a peak. But that's all.

There is a very fine line between looking sensual (remember, that is the key word) and looking cheap. A Latin woman wants by all means to look sensual. We are proud of our bodies, but like anything you are proud of, you also want to be careful.

Here again I believe that the two-inch rule applies. Push your breasts together. When you start to see cleavage, measure two inches down. That is the absolute maximum that they should show. The rest, my friends, is for the bedroom, not for massive consumption.

Having said that, there is another aspect of your presentation where I encourage you to throw caution to the wind. Yes, I know, I'm asking you to be a lady, but under that proper dress you should wear the sexiest underwear you can find. Perhaps not Fredericks of Hollywood, but definitely Victoria Secret, and if your budget allows it, French silk. You can leave the Calvin Klein cotton hip huggers to go to the gym, but when you are with a man the packaging is of utmost importance. The mere fact that you're wearing a body-hugging tanga, which by the way was invented in the beaches of Rio, where people literally worship the female body, will make you feel sexy (all that friction.) In fact it was Brazil's top plastic surgeon, Ivo Pitanguy, the one who developed the procedure for the thigh and fanny lift, such is the Brazilian preoccupation with female beauty. A stroll through the beautiful beaches of Copacabana, in the Brazilian capital, will reveal mostly taut, bronzed bodies playing in the sun any day of the week. (I have yet to figure out when it is that they go to work.)

Let your man take a peak at a lacy brassiere, but just a peak, mind you. Remember that absolutely only the lacy part should show in a discreet manner, perhaps when you're leaning forward. Once you have established a relationship and are farther advanced in your intimacy, find a black bustier with garter belts and wear it with old-fashioned stockings. Yes, the ones you have to pull up one by one.

A man once told me that the biggest sin modern technology committed against sensuality was the invention of the pantyhose. I'm not telling you to clean out your drawers and wear only stockings, but save a pair for a special occasion—and take them off slowly and deliberately when you want to delight your man. If something is guaranteed to spice up your love life, that is. It goes back to the Victorian era, when any allusion to sex was taboo and corseted ladies populated men's fantasies. Remember what happened to liquor consumption during Prohibition? Yes, the same thing happened to sex during Victorian times!

By wearing sexy undergarments you will become part of his fantasy world. It boils down to men being the incredibly visual creatures that they are. Men have sexual thoughts at an average of every fifteen minutes. Don't you want to be the one he thinks of when he fantasizes? So the formula is quite simple, ladylike on the outside and naughty inside. Women tell me that the mere fact that they are wearing beautiful, lacy lingerie makes them feel deliciously sensual. There is no arguing that silk feels wonderful on your naked body, and when you feel that way, your femininity quotient goes up several notches and your man has no choice but to catch your fire.

You Can't Tuck in Your Hips

Wouldn't it be wonderful if we could? Now picture this: You've just spotted the perfect slinky black jersey dress you have been looking for. The one you're sure will make you look like Angelina when she's not pregnant. You rush into the dressing room of Bloomies and, bless the dressing room fairies! it slides right on. So far so good.....You tuck in your tummy and face the mirror, but wait, what is that prominent arch going from your waist to your thighs? Hips, time two. Let's face it girls, Latin women got hips. And while curves are feminine, too much of a good thing is not a good thing. For Anglo-Saxon women this seems to be less of a problem, but as time goes by staying slim seems to be a universal challenge.

What's a girl to do short of starving herself and slaving at the gym? The good news is that you can still eat all the things you like and keep calories under control—with some variations. Such as:

Substitute brown rice for white rice. It will stay longer in your tummy and keep you satisfied until your next meal. The reason is that the hull (the outer covering of the grain that gives it the dark color) is left intact and your stomach needs to work double time to break it down. And guess what? As long as your stomach is working, you're not hungry. You only get into trouble when it has nothing to do. That is why the more unprocessed foods we eat, the better off we are. The same applies to bread and pasta. Buy whole grain whenever possible; you will love the nutty flavor and will also derive all the nutritional richness of the intact grain. Better yet, try quinoa, a berry that could pass for a grain, cultivated in the high Andes that is now available in national health food stores like Whole Foods Market. Quinoa looks like cous cous when cooked and has a very high protein content, making it an ideal side dish.

Reduce your intake of potatoes—and avoid the fried ones at all cost! When I interviewed Miami cardiologist Dr. Arthur Agatston, just before he launched

The South Beach Diet, he told me something I have never forgotten, and I want to pass that information on to you: "If you eat a mound of French fries, you might as well ingest a big lump of sugar." Fries metabolize into the white stuff quicker than you can say "fast food." If you love potatoes, try baking them, scoop out the inside, leaving about ½ inch in, spray with cooking spray and bake at 400 degrees until crisp. Same potato flavor with a portion of the calories. Or better yet, eat sweet potatoes instead. They are loaded with vitamin A and fiber and have a much lower sugar content.

Grill, microwave or steam instead of frying. Tostones are fried green bananas that Latins eat instead of French fries. The bad news is that they need to be fried twice. First, to soften them to be able to mash them, after which they're fried a second time to crisp them. Think of all that oil and extra calories that are going to sit right on your hips.

Try instead to microwave them to soften them and grill them to crisp. You can do the same thing with potatoes, by the way. The end result is very similar to the real thing with zero oil, and you still get the benefit of the fiber to help keep you clean inside, and a good helping of potassium for extra energy.

Turn vegetables into your friends. Learn how to cook vegetables in a way that will make them appetizing. My introduction to veggies was a boiled Succotash my mother used to buy in the freezer section of the supermarket when we first came to Miami. It took me another ten years to discover ways to prepare and love vegetables, which provide most of your vitamins and fiber. They can also fill you up with minimum calories. Some of my favorite ways to enjoy vegetables are:

Roasted with a drizzle of olive oil.
Chopped up in a salad bowl for a delicious summer lunch, the more the merrier. Pick brightly colored veggies—the brighter the color, the more loaded they are with antioxidants.
Sautéed with garlic and olive oil
Pureed in a satisfying soup

Eat fruit and low-cal Jell-O for dessert instead of sugary confections. Aside from empty calories, sugar will give your metabolism a sudden energy rush before crashing and making you feel even hungrier half an hour later. Fruits are chock-full of vitamins and anti-oxidants (the stuff that keeps your cells young)

Stop eating when you stop feeling hungry. Anything you put into your mouth after that is recreation...and I can think of better things you can do for entertainment. If you just follow these six steps I promise those bulges will slowly melt into the lovely curves you always wanted.

Grooming

God gave you a face. I hope for your sake, it is a beautiful one. But very few women over forty, and most of the ones before that age, look their best without makeup. A Latin woman knows that, and she excels at the art of applying makeup. We absorb this knowledge with our mother's milk. And it extends to manicures and pedicures. In short, anything that makes a woman more like a woman and less like a man. Again, it has to do with those wonderful differences!

I remember being about six years old when we lived in a big apartment in Old Havana. My mother was pregnant with my brother and she couldn't get out much since she was having a difficult pregnancy.

Every week like clockwork, during those nine months, a manicurist would come in to do my mother's nails, and that of her two cousins. That is probably one of the images which became imprinted on my mind from my early childhood.

The woman would come in carrying a black attaché case, very similar to a doctor's bag. She would set it down on the dining room table, spread out a towel and start to take out the manicure instruments—which she would sterilize with alcohol-infused cotton balls before starting to trim my mother's cuticles. After that she would begin to file her nails and —this was the best part—one by one out of that bag would come the colorful bottles of nail lacquer: bright deep reds, pearly whites, shy pinks. My mother would choose one —depending on her mood and what was going on during the week she would invariably choose either a bright red or a soft pink—and the manicurist would begin applying the color in careful strokes.

I used to enjoy even more watching as she did the nails of my mother's cousin Lillian. Hers were much longer and she would trace a half moon at the bottom and fill it in with white pearl lacquer, painting the rest in a deep blood red. I would stand very quietly next to the manicurist, mesmerized by her artistic endeavor until every nail was polished and once, even sneaked in a few strokes of lacquer on my own short little nails. Such ecstasy!

At that very young age I became addicted to the beauty rituals that go hand in hand with being a Latin woman, and I must say that at the ripe old age of (I'm not gonna tell you) I still take great pride in my appearance—and so do all of my friends. I know one of them from the time we were in kindergarten and you can tell it's Thursday by her beauty shop appointment. Call us shallow if you wish, but Latin women will economize in anything else but their beauty rituals.

And since we're on the subject of nails, the best way to keep yours from breaking is to keep them moisturized. Yes, even the toughest nail hardeners won't do a good job if your nails are dry and brittle. I have found that cocoa butter does the job for me. Rub it on the nail bed and cuticles to keep them soft and supple and watch your nails grow. Cocoa butter is also a godsend to keep the sole of your feet from getting calloused between pedicures.

Your Fragrance

The first time I danced with my husband he stepped back, breathed in and looking dreamily at me exclaimed: "you smell like a flower." Perfume is something that I can't live without and is part of my daily beauty ritual. Perfume should be applied in layers, to make it last longer. I shower, dab on a perfumed body lotion and finish with a spray of the same perfume. I usually stick to one for months, even years. It becomes my signature.

Smell is the sense most closely associated with memory. A favorite fragrance can evoke all sorts of forgotten experiences, bringing them to life as if it were yesterday. Just close your eyes and take a whiff of the first cologne you ever wore and see what happens.

You'll probably go back to the time when you were fifteen—high school crushes and all.

Well, guess what? The same thing is going to happen to him if you are partial to, say, *Angel*, and he happens to pass by a counter where they are testing it on customers.

You are going to pop into his mind. But also whatever was going on between the two of you when you were wearing it. Isn't that wonderful?

I have a rule: I never buy my own perfume. Why? Partially for the same reasons explained above. Because fragrance is something so personal, I like to wear one that has been picked out by the man in my life. After all, he's the one who is going to smell it on me. Isn't he? So he might as well smell one he likes. I think perfume is the most sensual gift a man can give a woman, for when she wears it, it creates a special bond between them.

I want my perfume to embody my true essence and to become thus embedded in his mind; to be part of what defines me when he thinks of me. And it makes me feel appreciated and special to receive a gift of perfume. So far I have never had to buy my own—and I hope to be blessed enough to be able to keep it that way.

For your own sake, I hope that is the case, but if there is no special man in your life right now, go out and buy the most seductive perfume you can find. I prefer to stick to florals, I personally don't like heavy, spicy scents, but to each his (or her) own. Dab it on the pulse points: behind your ears, on your wrists and breasts, or spray a fine mist all over whenever you go out, even if it's just to the grocery store. Don't be surprised if the boy at the checkout counter insists on carrying out your packages—and even refuses the tip!

One of my earliest memories of perfume goes back to the time when I was a teenager. My boyfriend had gone to Europe with his older brother in order to buy machinery for his father's factory while we were still living in Havana (which, as it turned out, Castro ended up keeping.) This was his first forage into the continent and the first time we were separated for an extended period of time. As a souvenir from his trip he brought me a beautiful crystal bottle of French perfume, which I proudly displayed on my night table, and I used to dab a bit of the fragrance behind my ears every time we met.

Even as teenagers ours had always been a volatile relationship, and shortly after his return we had a big fight. Such was my rage that I threw the entire contents of the bottle down the toilet. Needless to say for several weeks after that incident, every time I flushed, the whole house smelled of Channel Number 5. (He had gotten me the very expensive extract, which is extremely long-lasting.) My bathroom, as you can imagine, became the most popular room in the house until we eventually made up and he bought me another bottle, but he never forgave me for throwing away his perfume, *and my bathroom never smelled that good again.*

Think of your favorite fragrance as your own good-will ambassador. It will reach someone's senses before you do, and even linger for a while. Have you ever gotten into an elevator, smelled a wonderful scent and wondered who was it that had just stepped out? Well then. You need all the help you can get. We all do.

Your Voice

Let's start with what we hear. I don't know about you. But for me, listening to a man's voice is as important as what he says. A deep, modulated voice is a sign of virility. Talking on the phone with a man who has this kind of voice is like a lover's caress to my ears. And in fact, a man with a deep voice has a higher level of testosterone, the male hormone. So be aware, this could be a good warning sign before getting to know a man better. If he sounds like your fifteen-year-old brother before he changed his voice, beware!

By the same token, you should be conscious of your voice when talking to him. The most seductive women I know talk to their men as if they were about to deliver the most intimate secret. There are two advantages to this. First, you will establish an immediate rapport with your man. It's as if you're saying: "this is just between you and me." Secondly, no matter what he's doing, you will catch his attention. Have you ever noticed how everyone strains to hear what you have to say when you whisper?

I have a friend who has the habit of saying whatever she has to say as if it were her most precious confidence. The end result is that at the end of a conversation with Amalia you feel grateful and chosen, as if she has confided in you as she only would with a very close friend.

Lastly, your voice will come out softer and sexier, no matter what you're saying. Now, lower your voice and repeat after me: "I have to do laundry tonight..." "I have to do laundry tonight..." See what I mean? So practice, practice, practice. There is nothing a man hates more than a high pitched voice. I have known grown men to run away from home for that reason alone. It reminds them of their mother yelling at them! So from now on think in terms of lowering your pitch and raising your love profile. Think of Jennifer Lopez whispering dancing instructions to Richard Gere in *Shall we Dance*?

2

Falling in Love Should be Fun

But let's go back to the main subject, which is the relationship between a man and a woman. When a man spots a woman he wants, his primal hunter instinct awakens and the pursuit begins. The first encounter is full of the wonder of discovery and unfulfilled fantasies. He likes the way she looks, the way she moves, the way she talks and carries herself. First encounters are full of subliminal impressions that impact us without us even knowing why. In reality they go back to the animal world. Have you ever noticed how animals sniff each other before they copulate? Would you believe that the way a person smells has a lot to do with his or her attractiveness to his/her mate? I would go beyond that to say that there is a certain energy each person radiates and, at least for me, that is the key to whether or not I feel attracted. The way a man looks at a woman, his longing for her and his passion for life —and her— are high on my list of priorities. You could be swayed by his looks or his intellect—attraction is such a personal thing!

Now let's go back for a moment to our friend the hunter. His primal instinct has been awakened and he's ready for the pursuit. Could this be the woman he has been waiting for? His heart aflutter he begins to line up his arsenal. One by one he starts firing up his weapons: The following phone call, peppered with innuendos where he begins to test her receptivity, the flowers... the invitation to a romantic restaurant by the water where he will wine and dine her... the soulful conversations over the telephone just before she goes to sleep...

He knows she will succumb, it's only a matter of time. But wait, she's not ready. Is it too soon? Her heart is not in it yet. His heart is not in it yet...she fires; he retreats. What now? Should he go into plan B? Does he have a plan B? Should he wait it out? Should she give in? Will she lose him if she does? Will she lose him if she doesn't?

Seduction is a game with its own rules. Those who know how to play it have an advantage, and that is what this book is going to give you: the time-tested, subtle tools that Latin women have been using almost instinctively over the years to make the man they truly desire fall head over heels in love with them. Now, play fair, for the object of the game should be not only to seduce, but hopefully to fall in love. So please, only use your newfound powers on someone you could truly love.

Now let's get to work. To win the heart of the man you want you have to start by being in the right place at the right time. So get up from the sofa and pick up the telephone. You are about to start putting together your social calendar. You don't have to be a socialite to start weaving a series of engagements. Suppose there are no dazzling parties you have been invited to. So what? That will come later. Right now a girl's got to eat, right?

Let's start with lunch. Just like you want to be selective about whom you date, you want to be selective as to where you eat. Pick a popular spot where professional men take their clients. This way you get double exposure (the professional—and his client) or a private club—if you don't belong to one, pick a girlfriend who does and go together

Where you sit is also important. We're talking strategy here, so choose a table in the middle of the room—the more people see you, and the more you can see, the better. A table tucked in a corner might be good for a heart-to-heart with your girlfriend, but it will certainly not advance your social life.

Once you're comfortably ensconced at your table of choice start by charming the waiter; he can be your ally in the next step, which is to find out who's who in the room. If all this sounds too calculating, remember you are just setting the stage. The real drama will come later, once you have spotted the object of your affection, and that is where the real you has to shine. For now you are just a stage director.

Part of that role is to put the waiter at ease. You want him to be your friend, remember? So make a few comments about the restaurant, find out which dishes he really likes and then order drinks and perhaps a small salad. We have to keep calories down and if you're going to eat out a lot you better watch it. A drink, on the other hand, gives you something to hold and play with while you talk. It doesn't have to be anything alcoholic, but it should look good. Even if you're just drinking iced tea, ask the waiter to bring it in a goblet. You can roll the stemware playfully between your fingers, which you can't do with a glass. Remember, a girl who's animated, happy and talkative will become a magnet for the attention of anyone entering the room. If you're just sitting there like a dead lox you might as well stay home and eat a sandwich!

But wait, a well-dressed, good looking man has just come in carrying a briefcase, accompanied by two other men. And lo and behold, the waiter has just escorted them to the next table. See what I meant by charming the waiter?

Now, what do you do? First of all, continue your conversation. He doesn't have to know that he's the best-looking piece of manhood you have seen in months and your heart is trying to make a quick exit through your mouth. You are calm and collected. Perhaps you give him a quick once-over and, if you're daring enough, a subtle nod. You examine your salad for a clue to your life's meaning as if it were a Ouija board and keep talking to your friend. Ask her a question and look in his direction. Go back to your food.

After a few more minutes of this, you look at him intently until he catches your gaze. At this point you should disengage and concentrate on your food again. Examine closely that piece of arugula you are about to put in your mouth, but throw a sideway glance at him before swallowing with satisfaction. A Latin woman enjoys everything with a passion, including her food. Mmm...he will catch on!

Now switch your attention back to your girlfriend; this is a good time to tell her a funny story and make her laugh. Look at him from the corner of your eye. You will see that he is straining to hear the conversation. Toss your hair, look him in the eye and smile demurely. If he doesn't get up and asks to join you, he's either married and faithful, gay, or has to report to his parole officer.

Trust me on this one. There is nothing more seductive to a man, or anyone for that matter, than a happy girl. Remember that old line "cry and you'll cry alone. Laugh and the world will laugh with you." Well. First, find enough reasons to be happy. Secondly, share that happiness with as many people as you can. One of them might just be the next man in your life.

My friend Serena was recently talking to a high-profile trial lawyer to whom she had just been introduced. When she asked him how long he had been divorced he changed the subject. After this happened three times during the conversation, she looked him in the eye and asked him point blank whether he harbored a dark secret about his previous marriage.

The man blushed and admitted that he had been divorced for thirty years.

"Thirty years!" exclaimed Serena, laughing. "You should throw yourself an anniversary party. I don't know too many men who have managed to stay single that long!"

"You mean you're not put off by that," he asked, relieved. "I admire your sense of humor. Most women run in the opposite direction when I tell them."

"Well. I'll tell you," Serena answered with a toss of her shoulder-length auburn hair. "This is the way I see it: we all make choices, and if you have stayed single this long it's because you're having a helluva good time, so let's drink to that!"

At the end of the evening the man invited Serena out for that Saturday night and once he let his guard down, felt so comfortable with her that he asked her to be his guest at his office Christmas party. What I'm trying to illustrate is that what goes on between a man and a woman should be fun. From that first look at each other, the first email, or the first tidbits of conversation, a Latin woman never forgets that there is an element of mischief in what is going on between her and the object of her affection. Perhaps because many of us grew up in countries where not too long ago we still needed a chaperone to keep an eye on us, what goes on between a man and a woman is still tinged with a touch of the illicit. Remember, they never trusted us. That's why we needed the chaperone in the first place! And isn't that delicious? Those furtive glances, that dazzling smile are like neon signs to a man proclaiming that we find him irresistible enough to do something naughty.

I would like to elaborate on this point. Have you ever made love in a place where you could be found out? Like in a beach or the back seat of a car? Remember the excitement? Now compare that with making love in the privacy of your own bedroom. There's no denying that passion is passion. You will love him to pieces wherever you happen to be, but knowing that someone, somewhere, could come in any minute and spoil your fun adds a sense of immediacy to your lovemaking, as if your feeling dial had just been turned up to the max.

Many years ago, too many to count, really, I was invited to the sweet sixteen party of a girlfriend at the famous Tropicana nightclub in Havana. A veritable monument to the excesses of pre-Castro Cuba, Tropicana was set in the middle of a lush tropical forest. The show, which rivaled the one at the Paris Lido, was chockfull of scantily dressed showgirls who slithered and danced on catwalks which hung firmly between the branches of huge trees. Sort of an eco-friendly Las Vegas.

The entire show was held outdoors where you could enjoy the caress of the balmy breezes. And what if it rained? The owners of the famous cabaret had thought of everything even back in the 50's, when Tropicana was built. In bad weather, big Plexiglas arches closed over the trees and the air conditioning kicked in while the showgirls didn't miss a beat. After the show, everyone went crazy dancing to the tunes of the fabulous Aragon Orchestra. Age limits were much more relaxed in Havana when it came to dispensing alcoholic beverages and it wasn't unusual for very young couples to partake of the show.

The night that I'm talking about, there was a group of four young couples next to our table who were sharing one chaperone. (This was usually the case, somebody's grandmother or elderly aunt would volunteer to make sure no improprieties were committed for the evening while the parents waited at home.) This particular evening the chaperone must have had had one drink too many, and by the stroke of midnight, when the show was over and the orchestra started to play, she fell asleep. A few minutes later the table was deserted ...except for the snoring chaperone.

Almost an hour went by before the couples began filing in again and all were seated in their respective places- the girls hurriedly retouching their lipstick and the boys straightening up their ties- by the time one of the girls tactfully woke up the chaperone, who nodded sheepishly and rounded up the couples for the trip back home.

Had she suspected anything? Maybe. But appearances were kept and who knows, maybe on the way home she remembered her own long-forgotten peccadillo way back when. But I can assure you that whatever happened behind those bushes was imprinted with the flavor of heightened excitement and fun. Those kids went home knowing that whatever happens between a man and a woman is a bit mischievous, but also precious, and worth taking a risk for.

Forget the Drama

I said bef°ore that falling in love should be fun. When you talk to a man let him know that you are having as much fun at this as he (hopefully) is. A Latin woman never forgets it. She enjoys the process as much as the end result. And if what you're looking for is marriage and commitment, the more important it is to emphasize the fun part of the courtship. After all, your mother was right when she told you that these are the best times, before the kids and the mortgage come into play. But, and this can't be οemphasized enough, contrary to what you might think, men are the true romantics.

Yes, women cry at weddings and follow the love stories of their favorite soap opera, but men, who face the practicalities of life on a daily basis—the company budget that needs to be balanced, the new contract that needs to be signed—need something more. They crave, like a breath of fresh air, the fun, lighthearted, free-spirited part of life that only a woman can bring into theirs. They treasure this kind of escape like a well-polished jewel they keep aside to enjoy at the end of a long working day. And a woman who is aware of this fact is truly precious.

A friend of mine often said: "If you leave a man alone he gets thoroughly bored. All a man knows how to do is work, discuss politics or watch sports." They need a woman to bring lightness into their lives. The time they spend with a woman is the only time that allows them to let go and feel, the time to be happy, and yes, romantic and carefree.

Even if you think your man is not romantic because he doesn't send you flowers or leaves little notes tucked under your pillow, if he teases you and laughs with you, and spends time just unwinding with you, he is placing you in a different dimension, one that belongs only to the two of you. That is romantic. A Latin woman will make sure to carve a few hours out of every day to just *be* with her man.

To most men, women are divine creatures that allow them to escape the stress of their daily grind, and the more successful and involved a man is with his work, the more he will appreciate what the right woman can bring into his life. A woman who understands this has a big advantage over all the others. Men get into a relationship for sheer enjoyment, for the pleasure of it. Believe me when I tell you that men are not hearing wedding bells when they see a woman they like. They just charge ahead with one goal in mind: to conquer her, while many women see a relationship as a means to an end... and that is where they fail miserably.

A woman who can greet her man at the end of a hard day's work with a soothing word, a kiss and a neck rub is worth her weight in gold and will never want for male companionship. And if she can make him laugh, she will earn a few hundred extra points. She's aligning herself with the time-tested balance of ying and yang, the female and male energies that complement each other. Ying: the receptive energy of the universe and yang: the active, aggressive male energy that it always attracts. If she's married, she is insuring her marriage against any outside influences by providing an oasis of lightness and calm that her husband will want to come back to time and again.

What happens during the time of courtship is also extremely important. This is when both lovers will test their affinity and will evaluate whether or not they have a future together. But they are treading on dangerous ground. At this point they are still strangers who are getting to know each other and many a misstep could be misinterpreted and easily turn into a disaster. This is when many women make the mistake of playing their cards too soon. They are primed for the kill when they should coast for a while.

A Latin woman truly enjoys the process of courting—or shall we say being courted—for the process itself. She enjoys talking to her man, the anticipation of seeing him, shopping and getting ready for that first date, the beauty rituals: the hair, the makeup, choosing the right perfume. Oh mercy, the fun of it all!

The other good stuff: the engagement ring, the wedding party, the house and the country club will come in due time, but a Latin woman is focused on the now: the sheer delight of meeting her man tonight, the first kiss of the evening that will make her heart race and her legs weak. The conversation over dinner peppered with innuendos... Let's face it, us girls from South of the border are passionate creatures... And men love it. So let your thunder sound tonight. He'll never get enough of you, I promise.

Madonna may be "the material girl," but she comes through as a tough cookie, while Jennifer Lopez and Penelope Cruz epitomize Latin femininity. They're both beautiful, curvy women and looking at them you can see that they keep fit: they visit the gym, but they don't live in it. Their bodies are taut and firm, but there is plenty of softness where it counts.

And speaking of softness. That is another attribute that a Latin woman values. The soft, maternal side of us is very close to the surface. Contrary to what many people think, the typical Latin woman is not a fiery Sophia Loren type. Unless we are driven to distraction by an uncaring man, we prefer to settle our differences within the boundaries of an embrace.

Latin men are macho and we encourage the positive side of that quality. Simply put, we let them be men. We don't pal around with our men, we don't try to fix the leaky faucet or look under the hood when the car doesn't start. Instead we let them do what they do best, and we concentrate on what we can do better. Men are territorial by nature and if you respect their terrain and maintain the healthy tension that should always exist between the sexes you will end up with a happier mate—and a more virile lover to boot.

A Latin woman also recognizes the importance of verbal foreplay. By that I mean the bantering that goes on between a man and a woman during the early stages of getting to know each other. "A Latin woman never goes straight to the point," says Gladys, an event planner married to a Latin man. "She will skirt the issue of lovemaking, but always maneuver the conversation so that it stays close to it, but never out of the limits of propriety. This way her man is always kept guessing as to whether she meant it or not."

The best analogy is to imagine you are going to a business meeting. Instead of getting straight to the point and try to close the deal, in Latin countries you will sip some *cafecito*, inquire about your client's family and share a few jokes before broaching the subject at hand. So will a Latin woman who is engaging a man she is interested in. She will inquire about his background to get to know him better, test his knowledge of current world issues to evaluate his level of sophistication, and finally entertain him with innuendos and double-entendres during dinner and in late-hour conversations over the telephone, but no more.

This will go on for several weeks and sometimes even months before getting to the point where she feels comfortable enough with him to get more personal. In Latin countries people know each other sometimes from the time they're born and there is less mobility, so they tend to stay in the same circles most of their lives. As a result introductions are made by friends or family, which places some expectations as to how a man and a woman should behave with each other.

In the U.S. we tend to date perfect strangers, which sometimes makes it easier to be more daring. We could always hide under the cloak of anonymity, knowing that there is a high probability we may never run into that person again for the rest of our lives if things don't work out, and don't need to explain to aunt Sophie that her neighbor's son bored us to death, even though he carries a PhD in Quantum Physics.

The flip side of that situation is that, not having the benefit of a proper introduction by old friends or family, we are taking the chance of going out with someone not appropriate for us or even worse, plain dangerous. Therefore it is even more important to tread carefully in order to avoid unpleasant consequences. Besides, by taking the indirect approach a woman is always titillating, but never improper or—God forbid—vulgar. Remember, always a lady!... but who ever said that ladies can't be fun?

3

Cook for Him

Since we're talking of sensuality, one of the most delightful pleasures humans can engage in has to do with the palate. Yes, eating is one of life's great pleasures. It is no coincidence that a man will "wine and dine" a woman he's interested in. Pleasures of the palate seem to be preliminary to other kinds of pleasures. And many a romance has been ushered in by a delightful evening of food and wine. Think in terms of Roman bacchanals, with tables laden with all kinds of delicacies. Or that great movie scene of Tom Jones slowly enjoying a leg of lamb, savoring every bite as he twists the bone around his eager fingers before licking them in obvious delight.

That scene alone should have given you a clue to the sensual nature of his character. Show me a man who enjoys the nuances of taste and I can almost place a bet on the quality of his lovemaking. I could be wrong, but this is a very good indicator. And please don't confuse enjoyment with appetite. If he suggests an "all you can eat" buffet on your first date and then goes back three times for refills, forget him. We're talking discernment here, an ability to appreciate quality in all the good things in life, not gluttony—God forbid. You want to stay away from any kind of unhealthy habits.

Latins have always recognized the link between good food and romance, and our movies weave eating and cooking into wonderful love stories. My two favorite ones are *Like Water for Chocolate* and *Doña Flor and Her Two Husbands*. This last one, a classic Brazilian film featuring a young Sonia Braga, is the story of a cooking instructor who ekes out a living by teaching her students how to prepare the typical dishes of Bahia, a romantic city on the Northeast coast of Brazil. In scene after wonderful scene, while she slowly sautees and simmers against the lush background of Bahia, her thoughts invariably fly out to Vadiño, the loose, bon vivant husband she adores. Both movies depict women lovingly cooking for their men, infusing their food with the love and yearning that they feel for them.

I know, you are going to tell me that in today's society women are too busy to cook. I don't mean to go back to the days when our mothers told us that the way to a man's heart is through his stomach. If he really loves you he won't mind if you can't fry and egg, and all that. But being a good cook is a definite plus that will be much appreciated. You don't have to do it on a daily basis, but at least set aside one day a week to cook him a splendid dinner. And do it with love. He will know the difference, and will elevate you to a special plane. Just think of him smiling as he listens to his poor friends' stories about women who won't cook, while he's married to a Goddess.

Here are some Latin dishes you can try the next time you cook for your man. And don't forget to open a bottle of wine to go with it: "One of the necessities of life," as Ivan, a thoroughly romantic Latin man calls it.

Peruvians and Mexicans have different versions of ceviche, a marinated raw fish dish that is the equivalent of the herring that is served in the Nordic countries. I prefer the Mexican version, which concentrates on fish or seafood. The Peruvian version adds sweet potato and corn, which I believe don't go well with the raw fish. (You can also make shrimp ceviche using the same recipe, or a mix of shrimp and fish.) This is a very easy dish to prepare. The key is using the freshest fish possible. The best ceviche I ever tasted was at the pier of San Luis

Obispo, a California seaside town where the fish was just caught and the ceviche was served over crispy tortillas. Mmm! It is also a wonderful dish to serve to someone who is watching his diet, for it is pure protein.

Fish ceviche
3 fresh fillets of tilapia, or any white fish
juice of 3 lemons
1 small onion
1 chopped tomato
¼ cup cilantro, chopped fine

Chop fish, tomatoes and onions and marinade for an hour in lemon juice.
Add cilantro and serve.

The key to this elegant salmon dish is the sauce. Argentines use it on their meat, but I found it equally delightful on salmon. You can also buy the sauce ready-made in Hispanic markets

Salmon with chimichurri sauce

2 pounds fresh salmon
salt to taste
chimichurri sauce

Sauce:

1 cup fresh parsley
1/3 cup olive oil
1 tbsp. red wine vinegar
1 tsp. salt
½ tsp. minced garlic
½ tsp. Tabasco sauce (optional)

Sprinkle salmon lightly with salt. Cover with sauce and let it stand in the refrigerator for 30 minutes, setting aside about 1/3 of the sauce.

Bake at 375 degrees until done (approximately 25 minutes). Serve with extra sauce on the side.

The following is an extremely easy to prepare dip that you can whip up in minutes. The jalapeÐo adds zest, but you can do without it for an equally delicious dish.

Guacamole

I ripe avocado
¼ cup fresh lime juice
½ cup fresh cilantro
½ cup chopped onions
½ cup chopped tomatoes
I tsp salt

Scoop avocado and mash with a fork. Add the rest of the ingredients and blend until smooth. Serve as an appetizer with raw veggies or chips.

Arroz con pollo was the "company" dish that used to be served in Cuba. It is the equivalent of a Spanish paella, without the seafood.

Arroz con pollo

I chicken, cut in pieces
½ cup green peas
2 cups short-grain rice
¼ cup oil
2 tsp. salt
2 bouillon cubes
½ tsp. pepper
2 tbsp. tomato sauce
I onion, chopped, or I tbsp. dried onion flakes
2 garlic cloves, minced

I green pepper, chopped
I tsp. vinegar
4 cups water
I can red peppers
I can beer
Saffron or yellow food colorant

Sautee chicken quarts. Take chicken out and sautee onion, garlic and green peppers. Add tomato sauce, vinegar, salt and pepper. Add chicken and water and simmer until chicken is halfway done. Add the rice and the beer, cover and cook until rice is soft.

Add the green peas. Garnish with slices of red pepper and serve.

A simple, everyday dish that is economical and simply delicious, picadillo can be prepared with either ground beef or turkey. The flavor is in the sofrito, the sautéed onions, garlic and pepper that accompany many Cuban dishes.

Picadillo

2 pounds ground beef or turkey
2 small fresh tomatoes, chopped
I onion, chopped
I green pepper, chopped
2 garlic cloves, minced
I tsp. salt
½ tsp. pepper
I-16 ounce can tomato sauce
¼ cup dry white or cooking wine
2 tbsp. olive oil

Heat the oil and sautee the chopped onion, garlic and pepper. Add tomatoes and simmer until soft. Add the meat and brown, turning to mix it all well. Add the rest of the ingredients, cover and cook for about 20 minutes. Serve with white rice and black beans.

Black beans are chock full of fiber and when combined with white rice are a complete protein. The Cuban version is flavorful and a staple in the Cuban diet. It is the perfect complement to a hearty Cuban meal—and a definite man pleaser!

Cuban Black Bean Soup

3 cups black beans
10 cups water
2 onions, chopped
2 green peppers, chopped
4 garlic cloves, minced
1 laurel leaf
1 tbsp. salt
¼ tsp. pepper
1 tsp. oregano
1 tsp. cumin

Soak beans overnight with one onion and one green pepper, cut in half. The next morning, boil water and spoon out the foam. Lower heat and simmer until beans soften. Sautee garlic and half of the onion and green pepper until soft and add to the beans. Let it cook for another half an hour. To thicken, spoon out a big spoonful of beans with a bit of the liquid and put through food processor until creamed. Add to soup, mix well, simmer for another 20 minutes and serve. It can be prepared the day before and refrigerated. Black beans usually taste better the following day, when all the flavors have married well.

Here is a very simple dessert that will impress as well as delight your guests.

Flan

1 can condensed milk
1 can milk or soy milk
½ cup sugar
5 eggs

Burn the sugar in a small pan until it liquefies. Pour the caramel on the bottom of a small, deep Pyrex, moving the container until it is evenly covered by the caramel. Beat eggs, add condensed milk and regular milk. You can do this all in a food processor or blender. Pour mix on cooled mold and bake in *baine Marie* (placing the mold inside a water-covered bigger container) for about 50 minutes or until a toothpick comes out dry. Refrigerate until thoroughly cool. Take it out, run a dull knife around the borders of the mold, press a platter against it and unmold. Scrape the bottom of the mold until all the caramel covers the flan. Serve... and wait for the compliments!

Sangria is served in Spain to usher in the summer. It marries the flavors of fruit and wine in a delicious and refreshing drink. You can easily drink a whole pitcher with your meal. This recipe calls for red wine, which is used in the traditional sangria, but you can use white wine instead for delicious white version.

Sangria
1 bottle red wine
1 apple, seeded and peeled, chopped
2 peaches, peeled and chopped
2 tbsp. sugar
1 bottle of lemon-lime soda

Mix wine, fruit and sugar in a pitcher, cover and refrigerate for 6 hours or overnight. When ready to drink add the soda, some ice cubes, and serve.

The mojito is the drink of preference in Cuba. It is light, refreshing and simply delicious. I had my first mojito when I was sixteen, but the drink didn't capture America's fancy until Pierce Brosnan ordered it in a James Bond movie. Here is the recipe for a genuine mojito. The secret lies in using the best rum you can find—and make sure you crush the mint leaves so they thoroughly release their flavor. This recipe is for two.

Mojito

2.5 oz Bacardi rum

24 mint leaves
2 tbsp. sugar
1 oz. lime juice
4 oz. soda water

Pour the rum and lime juice in a shaker. Add mint leaves and sugar, crushing the mint thoroughly with a spoon. Add crushed ice and soda water. Serve in two glasses, garnish with a mint leaf and enjoy.

4

Flatter Him

Let's talk about this for a minute. Don't you feel flattered when a man thinks you're beautiful? Well then, men are just as vulnerable to flattery as you are. So be generous with your comments, but be honest. Don't tell him he's as eloquent as Barack Obama if he can barely string two sentences together (although I don't see how you could fall for an inarticulate man, I know I never could, but many women do.)

Remember when you first met him. There must have been something that attracted you to him in the first place. It could be his voice. It always works for me. I have been known to fall in love over the phone, although you have to be careful with that too. You see, women tend to fall in love with what they hear, while men fall in love with what they see. More on that later. Or it could be something as prosaic as his body or his dark curly hair. Whatever it is, highlight it. Make it a recurrent theme.

You could say something like "Yes, Paul tried to convince you that the energy crisis is here to stay, but you certainly pointed out the many ways in which we are developing alternative fuels. Your rhetoric was brilliant!" Or something as simple as: "I love that dimple in your chin. It drives me wild!"

I have a girlfriend whose boyfriend has spindly legs, but is blessed with a great torso, which she's always touching with obvious delight and commenting on. Needless to say Victor struts around with a shirt opened almost to his navel, an obviously happy man. Does she ever mention his legs? Of course not! She wants him happy.

Many years ago, in my teenage years, I once mentioned to a friend at our beach club that he had good legs. Believe me if I tell you, even today as a grandfather, whenever he sees me, he pulls up his pants bottoms to sneak in a glance at his hairy gams. Poor guys, I guess us girls really don't shower them with compliments about their anatomy, but contrary to what you might think, they are just as vain as we are, and grateful as hell for whatever we manage to dish out.

So go ahead and find whatever it is that sets your man apart and bring it up as often as you can, he'll love you for it. But whatever it is, tell the truth and be honest with your feelings. Don't tell him you find him irresistible if you don't feel it first. We're talking true love here. This is not a hobby, it's the real thing.

Listen to Him

There are few things a man enjoys more than to have the woman in his life listen to him. By that I mean really listen. Like you put everything on hold—your attempts at straightening out the house, checking your email or talking on the phone with your girlfriend—to give your full attention to what he has to say. Pay attention, for contrary to what you might think, your opinion counts. Ask questions, pretend you are an interviewer and really delve into the subject.

Being a good listener is a tremendous advantage for a woman who wants to conquer the mind of an intelligent man. Remember, sex he can always get, but the support and admiration of an equal is hard to find, and you want that equal to be you... so he doesn't have to go someplace else to find her.

If you value the kind of bond that only gets established between two people who can share not only a bed but also ideas, be generous with your attention and build him up. Yes, you heard me, even the most accomplished man, used to the validation of the rest of the world feels like a failure if he doesn't feel the admiration of his mate. My friend Maria, an enlightened Latin woman married to an extremely successful man, tells me that the more successful the man, the more ego boosting and admiration he will need from his woman. Turn the conversation to him. Powerful men are selfish, so learn to live with it if that's the kind of man you want, and capitalize on this knowledge. Empower him—it will get you anything you want.

If what you crave is just the opposite: someone who will be focused on you and shower you with compliments and encouragement that's fine, but go fishing in different waters. This kind of specimen lives in a different pond. Very few very successful men are also sensitive and giving. It just doesn't go with the territory. You have to be somewhat selfish and totally focused on your career in order to succeed. The giving and caring usually comes later in life, when he starts to plan for retirement, for this type of man. But regardless of what kind is in your life, build up his appeal as a man as well.

"I tell my husband constantly that he could get any woman he wants," Maria confesses playfully, "knowing that I think it is a distinct possibility seems to be enough for him. So far I have never found any evidence that he wants to prove my point, and I want to keep it that way..."

How many women do you know that do just the opposite? They get angry and frustrated with their men and constantly belittle them. Can you blame them when they go looking for gratification some place else? Often when you find out who the man replaced his wife or girlfriend with, you find someone less attractive and less obviously desirable. Nine times out of ten her secret weapon is that she knew how to build up a man who was starved for recognition. One man in my family almost left his wife for his much younger assistant. When I saw a picture of the girl in question I asked him what he saw in her. Aside from the age difference his wife was much prettier. "But she thought I was brilliant. Every word that came out of my mouth was like a crown jewel to her. She was great for my ego!" was his answer

So if you want to keep your man by your side, shower him with compliments, empower his virility, his intelligence and his accomplishments. You will not only gain a faithful companion, but a more potent lover as well.

5

Bring Spirituality into Your Relationship

We live in a materialistic world. We shop till we drop, drive fancy cars and try to keep up with the Joneses. That is why a woman who likes a man for what he is, is as refreshing as a breath of fresh air. We're not saying that you have to live a simple life with your beloved. There is an old Spanish saying: "With you, I don't mind eating bread and onions." I believe that is a bit extreme. After all, we like and need all the things we mentioned above (perfumes, manicures, etc. to be really happy.) But a man has to know that you like him first and whatever else he brings into your life second.

And that it where spirituality comes in. I have seen women who have lured powerful men away from their materialistic girlfriends by the simple virtue of liking them just for being men. Am I saying that you should reject everything else that kind of man brings into your life? By no means. That is certainly part of his allure. There is no more potent aphrodisiac than power and success, and if that is the kind of man you are aiming for, that is probably one of the main reasons you are attracted to him in the first place. I'm just saying that should not be the primary reason to fall in love with him.

If I have you thoroughly confused, let me explain. A spiritual woman will look first at the personality and appeal of the man, and everything else second. His station in life might be part of that appeal, but not the only reason. You may find yourself strongly attracted to his kindness, or his need for love and understanding.

I know a Latin woman who is presently dating a very eligible widower who is a financial advisor to high net worth individuals all over the world. The main reason she's seeing him? She finds him extremely warm and honest in his need for companionship. "The fact that he travels first class is a nice perk," she tells me, but I wouldn't marry him just for that."

I happen to know that she divorced her second husband because he was cold and distant (even though they also traveled first-class.) The man would go on business trips for several weeks and only call when he was ready to come home. "I'm not putting myself through that ordeal any more," she told me. "Human quality is much more important to me now." I guess given enough time, any girl can become wiser.

A spiritual woman will fall in love and be compassionate and loving towards her man, provided he can reciprocate. Don't waste all that warm and fuzzy loving and the good qualities that you can bring into a relationship with a dried-out business-obsessed money machine that can only give you things. Remember many high achievers get to where they are because they are exclusively focused on their careers and any woman in their lives will come in a distant second—or third.

I know a Latin woman who fell for such a man. From the very beginning of their marriage Eduardo was obsessed with furthering his business, working nights and weekends while Carmen tended to their home and their growing family. After fifteen years of very hard work Eduardo finally became extremely successful, selling his pharmaceutical business to a European consortium for several millions.

Would you believe that at that point he got involved with his secretary and sued for divorce? They were in the final stages of the litigation when he realized that his new-found love was requesting the same attention as his wife, and he came back to Carmen.

When asked why he did, his answer was cut and dry, like everything else in his life: "at least Carmen's nagging is by now familiar to me, and staying was a lot less expensive than going through with the divorce." Workaholics will buy you a beautiful home and perhaps important jewelry but remember that a diamond is a very cold stone and will never keep you warm at night as would a lover's embrace.

There are not too many high achievers who can really appreciate a woman for everything she can bring into their lives, so if you're lucky enough to find one with feelings, who can truly fall for you, cherish him. Let him know early on in the relationship that material things are not that important to you. He is. The warmth and excitement he brings into your life is what you truly treasure. Men of this caliber are not used to that behavior in the women they tend to associate with. He will respond... in spades.

Introduce Him To the Family

Latins are big on family values. We thrive on big, extended families and are very observant of traditions. As a result, if there is a new man in our life it is not long before he gets to meet, if not mom and pop right away, at least some of our family members. Brothers, sisters, cousins, nieces and nephews are usually in the picture and in and around our lives.

Call me old-fashioned, but I firmly believe that in this cold, rushed, materialistic world we live in, men still find comfort in a warm, embracing family. I remember a close friend who was not particularly attractive, but whose mother ended up luring her now husband by practically adopting him and showering him with good food and affection. More than thirty years later they are still happily married, and she, a successful real estate executive, still cooks the occasional dinner when they stay home.

Latins, as a whole, form strong attachments rather quickly. A cousin—whose son, a handsome and successful bachelor, dated many women over the many years of his happy bachelorhood—used to complain that she didn't want to meet any more girls until Marcos settled down. "I get attached to them. I can't help it," she used to tell me, "and then he stops seeing them. It hurts!" He finally found the woman of his dreams and brought her home to meet mother, but not before he had asked for her hand in marriage.

In these days of Internet dating, he met her in one of the big dating sites. Having dated many gorgeous women in Miami, and lasting only a few months with each one, (including one who actually helped him move into his new home before they broke off) he fell for this level-headed, smart financial analyst with short dark hair who blew him away with her keen mind and down-to-earth good family values. He flew to meet her in New York, where she lived then, and after a month of emails and constant telephone calls, being a true romantic Latin man, flooded her apartment with red roses before proposing. His father, a pediatrician and his now happy mother fly once a month from Miami to Los Angeles, where they now live, to see the grandchildren. We get attached. We're Latins. We can't help it.

6

Cultivate a Sense of Humor

*O*f sex is the lubricant that keeps the love machine humming, a good sense of humor keeps it tuned. A good joke at the right time or an irrelevant comment with the right intonation can dissipate pent-up anger and avoid an unnecessary argument.

A good friend of mine is married to a man who always has to be right. That is one non-negotiable issue in their marriage. Javier simply has to win every argument. Maria Eugenia, a smart Latin woman if there was ever one, has that situation covered. Javier and she were recently invited to a dinner party and when the day came, aware of the fact that she takes a long time getting ready and that their hostess is a stickler for punctuality, Maria Eugenia got an early start so that they could get there on time.

"What are you doing?" Javier asked her as she took out the outfit she was going to wear for a closer look, "it is only five thirty; the party doesn't start until eight."

"No, darling, I remember Celia saying it was at seven," she replied, taking the dress out of the plastic wrap where it had come from the cleaners.

"No, no, no, she said eight," Javier shot back as the vein in his right temple started to throb and she could see they were about to begin another ugly fight. At this point Maria Eugenia looked him in the eye and deadpanned:

"That's exactly what I meant, darling, eight o'clock, I'm going to lie down for an hour in the meantime."

At exactly six thirty she got up and carefully started applying her makeup. She got dressed at a leisurely pace and helped Javier with his tie as she usually does without another word about the time. By seven thirty they were out the door and got to the party at eight, like Javier had wished. Once they got in and realized that everybody had been there for an hour she let him in on her little game. He caught on, apologized for their tardiness to their hostess, gave a little nudge to Maria Eugenia under the table, and they were on time from then on. But more importantly, an ugly argument was avoided.

All cultures that have had to endure difficult times have always resorted to humor as a coping mechanism. But for Latins, being simpatico is non-negotiable and being "heavy" (lacking a sense of humor) is the one sin that is unforgivable. Javier, a true Latin man, was able to put aside his need to be right that one time and appreciated Maria Eugenia's little game for all it was worth, chuckling all the way home from the party.

Some of the most charming women I know are masters at finding humor in every situation. I know a lively, but heavy-set enchantress who snatched one of the most eligible bachelors of Puerto Rico with her irrepressible joie-de-vivre. At the ripe old age of sixty, Ernesto had never been married. A successful builder, he had dated San Juan's most beautiful showgirls until he met Susana.

They met in New York, where she worked for a high profile investment banker, when he came into his office to ask for a loan for a big project he was starting to develop in the outskirts of San Juan. He was to build over a hundred homes and Susana's boss was to provide the financing. The meeting took some time and being that Susana was the banker's right hand, she had to come into the office a few times in order to bring documents to be signed and serve coffee, and also had ample opportunity to look Ernesto over and display some of her terrific personality, which he didn't fail to appreciate.

At the end of the meeting, Ernesto had sealed a deal and made a date with Susana. He asked her out to lunch and she brought along her two young sons. Enchanted with her, he asked her again for dinner and she brought the two older siblings. Perplexed, he asked her "How many children do you have?" "Only two," she answered. "They grow fast!"

A month later she had moved to San Juan and six months later they were married... and he adopted her four children!

7

We've Got Rhythm

oie-de-vivre, translated from the French means "joy of living," a quality that seems synonymous with the Latin culture. It is reflected in our music, in our art and in the way we relate to others.

Music, for the Latin soul, is what religion is to the pious. It elevates, affirms us and transcends our daily hurts and worries. It is a small wonder that Latin music has so many aficionados. Having been born in Cuba, I am partial to the sultry Caribbean rhythms that were brought to our shores by the black slaves who came to work the sugar plantations. Cuban music has its origins in the liturgical sounds of the Lucumi religion prevalent in the Congo, from where most of Cuba's blacks originate. Over the years it blended with the Moorish-inspired cadence of Spanish songs to create the rhythmic bolero, cha-cha and salsa of today.

Latin parties need little more in the way of entertainment than a good band. Give us good music to dance by and we're in heaven. You will be hard-pressed to find a Latin woman who does not know how to dance. Although I'm sure you will find one here or there with a defective dancing gene, most of us learn to dance shortly after we learn how to walk. It simply goes with the territory. Part of it has to do with the fact that Latin girls are encouraged to use their bodies gracefully and take ballet and dancing lessons from the time they are very young, (I took ballet lessons from age nine to twelve, and only quit when I had to dance *en pointe* —on my toes.) My teacher, who was trained by Cuba's prima ballerina Alicia Alonso, insisted on her girls not using rabbit's fur as a cushion in their ballerina slippers as many dancers do, and it was just plain too painful. Part of it is the fact that music is an integral part of our lives and how we socialize.

If you don't relate well to music, I encourage you to take dance lessons. Not only will you learn how to dance and use your body in more expressive ways (all that swaying and shimmying can drive a man crazy and that, by the way, is some of the purpose of dancing—just think of the harem girls) but it is a wonderful way to meet men and socialize in a non-threatening, fun way.

Dancing also encourages body contact. You can learn more in five minutes about a man by the way he holds you—the feel of his hand on your waist, the pressure of his touch—than in a month of soul-searching conversations.

The way a man holds you in the dance floor is a metaphor for what you can expect later on in the bedroom—and in your life with him. Is his touch firm and strong, or weak and tentative? Is he good at leading you? Does he dance close to you or does he hold you at arm's length like my ex boyfriend used to? (a true relationship killer if there was ever one.) Or does he crave your closeness enough to dance cheek to cheek? My all time favorite! Do your steps and his mesh seamlessly, or do you find that you have to fight his clumsiness all through the song?

There is nothing more seductive than to dance close to your man to soft music. Skin to skin, body to body. Close your eyes for a moment and imagine the music engulfing both of you while you move in sync. Such heaven! I have always made dancing part of my love rituals and sharing songs part and parcel of my love language. There is a reason why couples often dance to "our song." That special tune, with its special words becomes a symbol of their love, and the words become encrypted in their love language for years to come. There is an extra bonus: every time he hears your song, it will become a reminder of you, wherever he happens to be. Think of it as insurance for your relationship. It works.

Dance with and for your man. Become his Scheherazade. Remember Jennifer Lopez practically seducing Richard Gere on the dance floor? Go ahead. You can do it. If nothing else you'll have a helluva good time while you try.

The way you walk

Our bodies were engineered for motion. And men and women move their bodies in different ways. Here we go again with those delicious differences! A man's walk is straight and determined. He knows where he's going and why. Think of a narrow-hipped Clint Eastwood approaching the bad guy in a western. Here comes the no-nonsense sheriff walking straight and tall with his gaze on his target, eyes ablaze with purpose and resolution.

A woman, on the other hand, should undulate as she walks. We've got hips (at least we Latin girls do—blame it on all those platters of beans and rice.) And try as we might to lose them it's always an uphill battle. So I say if you got them, whether or not you're Latin, flaunt them. Remember, we're not built like boys, *au contraire!*

I was once told by a male co-worker that I was the only person he knew who walked on ball bearings. When a Latin woman walks, she slides. There is a cadence that goes from her left foot and left hip to the right foot and right hip and is done leisurely, with the head held high. In the skinnier version, it ends up looking like a model's walk, but few of us are that slim.

This is the way women have walked for generations in the high Andes and the villages of Mexico and Central America carrying packages to the market on their heads, which forces them to keep their upper torso straight while the hips do their thing. (Try walking with a book on your head and it will automatically correct your posture.) The good news is that all that hip rotation is extremely sexy. (Remember Elvis?) You can do it a lot more discreetly, but do it any way you can and see what happens. With practice it will become second nature and once you master the movement you will end up with an unexpected bonus: you will become a natural at Latin dancing, since hip movement is the basis for most of the salsa moves. Are we having fun yet?

The "piropos"

Now I'm going to delve for the first time into the Latin man's territory. There is a delicious custom that is indigenous to Latin countries; albeit I'm afraid could be a dying art. I'm referring to the *piropo*. When an attractive woman used to walk down the streets of Madrid or Havana, men felt compelled to voice their admiration by coming up with their most poetic comments while the object of their desire passed by. If the girl was very young she would blush and walk faster, but the more seasoned women simply smiled, slowed their step and relished the minor commotion that formed on their wake—fanned by all that hip swaying!

Some of the most inspired *piropos* were real works of art, some were funny and all made everyone involved a little happier to be alive. My favorite: *"Girl, if you cook the way you walk, I'll clean up my plate!"*

Who knows, perhaps today such a thing could be construed as sexual harassment, but to my young ears they felt like a compliment to my budding womanhood. And I noticed in the eyes of the men who whispered them, when I dared to look, a special glint as they saw me blush. Did anybody get hurt? I don't think so.

They got their fun and I got my spirits lifted. But what's even more important, the game was on. They were doing what they do best: being men and I was learning, even at that tender age, how to be a woman. The polarization was as God had intended it to be. I would give anything to inspire a well-thought out, saucy *piropo* once again.

8

Let him Catch You...

And Take Care of Him When He Does

et's flash back for a moment to pre-historic times. Man is ready to leave his cave to go hunting. He will run, surprise and pummel his prey until he can safely take it home to feed the family. He walks through the cave's opening carrying his prize and he gets a hero's welcome. Wife and kids gather around him and he is toasted as the proud provider that he is. Life is good.

Over the ages this act has taken on different guises. Modern man puts on a suit and tie and goes to the office, but he's still ready to face the jungle out there and fight for his survival. The carrot at the end of the stick? The deal nobody else could close, the coveted piece of property that he can now not only derive a good income from, but also brag about what he had to go through to get and how he closed it. Life is good.

What are the implications of all this? Man is still turned on by pursuit. This is a fact that has been hard wired into his psyche through many generations of pursuers. Remember the survival of the fittest? Only those who made it through the ages are still here making sure their genes keep on being passed on. If your man is on Planet Earth, he is automatically one of the privileged ones that have survived through the ages. The descendant of that pre-historic cave-dweller who happily clobbered buffalo and lions after cunningly trapping them before finishing the hunt. Did his ancestors enjoy the whole bloody mess? You bet! Did the thrill of the hunt become engraved on his mind?

Right again!

So we have established an undisputable fact. Man likes to hunt. Man is the pursuer, and has been for ages. I don't know about you, but I prefer not to mess with Mother Nature. I say, if he likes to pursue, let him. The same instinctive process that drove him to trap that buffalo will lead him to want to trap you.

You are the trophy he wants to strive for, the reward so unique and wonderful that will show to the world he is capable of achieving anything he sets his sight on. Should you deny him that pleasure? Of course not. By letting him catch you, you are allowing your man to behave like one. Like so many generations of men have behaved through the ages, you are giving him the tools to become another member of the clan and proudly declare that he won you over. The harder the pursuit, the more he will prize you and the more he will brag to his friends about what he did to finally conquer you.

This is one fact that Latin women pride themselves in knowing. Men prefer to make the move. We let hem. We don't call, we don't directly approach. We don't speak to him first. We don't bake him cookies. At least not until he is safely ours. Fine, you may say. That's OK for the likes of Angelina and Heidi (Klum) who would probably have a line of men waiting for them to even glance at. But what about the rest of us plain mortals? How do we let him know that we simply occupy the same earthly space as he does? Simple. We wait. In the meantime we do other things, like:

We enroll in a gym and start working out with the best trainer we can find.
We start eating healthy and cut out bad carbs.
We join a discussion group and start honing in our political muscle by learning about issues and candidates.

We take a class on Quantum Physics. Just because we're curious.
We volunteer at the local hospital. Just because we care.

In short, we try to become the best human being we can possibly be. Because if you want to attract a terrific man, you have to start by becoming a terrific woman. If you are reading this book, you are motivated enough to find love in your life and are determined to do it the right way. By taking the time to make a change and the effort to make a difference.

If you align yourself with the right vibrations, you will attract like-minded people. Notice I used the word attract, which is key to this chapter. Attraction is a feminine energy. It is the action of bringing in, rather than going out and getting. This brings us back full cycle to where we started. Man the aggressor, man the pursuer. Woman the receiver, the welcoming, embracing force that is waiting for him at the end of the rainbow. You have become that very unique creature that he wants to conquer and bring home to his lair. Life is good. *Again.*

Long-distance Relationships

What if you fall in love with someone who lives in another town? Or another country? I have been known to fall head over heels for someone living in another continent! Long-distance relationships have their challenges. And their advantages:

You can keep going out with your girlfriends and live practically like a single girl while he's not around (except for dating—I believe in being true to one man.)
You can watch old movies all weekend or talk to your girlfriends whenever you want while keeping the threads of a relationship going, which I find very comforting.
The fact that somebody cares, wherever he happens to be, that we can keep an ongoing conversation through the miles is enough to keep me sane and happy for months at a time.
And the excitement of the reunions! You get off that plane and run to meet him, and there he is waiting for you with a bouquet of flowers, ready to whisk you to a romantic dinner by the water while you watch the sunset. Sheer heaven!

But will it last? Distance can be a killer. I have kept relationships long-distance for as long as two years, but constant contact is necessary, meaning we talk on the phone three to four times a day and email or text message like crazy. During those two years we were best confidants and discussed every detail of our days over the phone to the point that we were practically living together across a continent. But in the end one of us had to make the move and none wanted to relocate and, in my case, leave behind friends and family.

So I say, unless you're prepared to move, let him go. A long-distance relationship tends to give you a false sense of security, the illusion that someone is in your life, when in reality you are both alone.

I truly believe that if you find yourself falling for out of towners all the time, listen to your heart. It might be an indication that you really cherish your alone time more than togetherness. And if that is where you are now, that is also OK.

Coming out

When should you go public with your new love? *After he does.*

You are a discreet creature who has too much going on in her own life to give top priority to any relationship. Men are used to getting top billing in a woman's life. That is why when they find a woman who doesn't, they do a double take.

You are involved with your work. Your family. Your friends. Your social life. And they will support you through the good and lean times. That is the stuff your life is made of. Any man that comes in will have his place in your heart. But has to wait for his place in your life until you are ready.

And that will only happen when you are a big deal in his.

Until then you can tell your closest friends, but just in passing. Like: "I went out with Richard last night. Saw a great movie. He is such a gentleman. I really like his poise." Period. When he starts to talk about you to his friends, like: "And this is Rosanne." And *they* stop the conversation to say:

"So this is the famous Rosanne. He doesn't stop talking about you!" When he wants you to meet his partner, his mother, his kids, you know you're in.

That is when you make a dinner party and invite your closest couples to meet your new man. And make sure you instruct them beforehand not to say: "So I finally get to meet Richard. I've heard so much about you!" You want your friends to sound cool. You make the commotion with his. He, on the other hand, is going to be scrutinized and, if he's lucky, will pass the test with your friends and family.

This is important because the way you present yourself from the very beginning is the way you are going to be appreciated and treated later on. He has to know that he needs to jump through hoops to get you. That you are such a fantastic package that only a very lucky man—him—will be able to catch you and cherish you for the rest of his life. If you let him.

Baby Him When He's Sick

When you stand at the altar you will hear these words:

In sickness and in health. You should take them to heart. When your man is not feeling well he regresses to babyland. To the time when mother would make him chicken soup, cuddle him and read him a story.

I say, two out of three is all you can handle. But for heaven's sakes, this is the time to spoil him. So go ahead and make him the chicken soup (if you want to score really high, get the recipe from his mother) and love him to pieces. Whatever you do now by the way of spoiling him will be amplified tenfold in his perception, so be generous with your attention. Fluff up his pillow, screen his calls. Let him enjoy this quiet time. Sometimes illness is a warning that we have to slow down to catch our breath. If he is involved in a stressful business it often is the body's self-protective mechanism at work, prompting him to take some much needed time off in order to ward off a more serious problem.

The other side of this is that if you withhold your caring at this point, it can spell disaster. I know a successful attorney who divorced his beautiful young wife after she refused to nurse him during a bout of back pain. "If this is how she treats me now, imagine what will happen if I get really sick," he told me. There is just so far a pretty face will take you…

For a man to feel sick is a sign of weakness and vulnerability. To see that a woman is capable of loving him in that condition earns her big-time Brownie points. It means that she is there not only for the good times, but also to offer comfort and succor. This is the woman he will trust and stand by forever.

Trust me on this; unless you do something really bad later on to spoil things, it is almost a guarantee of his lasting commitment. So cuddle him, bring him dinner in bed, and rub his belly, his back or whatever else ails him. A Latin woman is not afraid to show her maternal side—and her man loves her for it. One of the happiest couples I know have been married for over forty years and they have always called each other "mami" and "papi." You see, in Spanish those are truly words of endearment.

9

Kids

His, yours and ours. Children are going to be part of your life with him. Whether this is a first marriage and you are starting a family or, more often than not, you are blending families, or living with his, or him living with yours, you are going to have children in your life.

There are times when a woman has to be a mother and a wife, and sometimes she has to choose between one and the other, according to the circumstances. Having been widowed at thirty six with two children, I often had to maneuver children and relationships and I can tell you, it is not an easy task. When my husband died my children were ten and fourteen and a hasty second marriage bit the dust due to the complexity of that situation. My new love lived in Los Angeles, the kids and I were in Miami. My son was ready to move. My teenage daughter wouldn't hear of leaving her friends behind.

In the end, he moved to Miami, but the stress of fitting into my life was too much and the marriage ended. I put my children first, and always have. Is that smart? I don't know, but that is the way it has always been for me. For my mother, however, it was quite different.

I left Havana in October of 1960 to stay with relatives in Miami. Shortly after, my parents and my brother joined me and we rented a furnished apartment in Miami Beach. We were all waiting for the Bay of Pigs invasion so that we could return to Cuba, and my father left the three of us in Miami to go back and try to salvage his business.

Needless to say, the invasion was a fiasco and he stayed on several more months to sell what he could and come back to us. But in the meantime, he didn't like staying alone and sent for my mother. What did she do? Pack her bags and go!

My brother and me, ages twelve and nineteen stayed alone in Miami for three months. Until my parents' return, I became the official head of household, holding a full-time job and learning how to cook and clean (something I had never done before) while I tried to take care of a twelve-year old boy.

The one good thing that came out of that experience is that I used my poor brother as a guinea pig to learn how to cook. The project would start with going to the market. Since we didn't own a car, I would walk and my brother would follow me in his bike so that he could help me carry the packages in the bike's basket back from the supermarket.

The cooking, unfortunately did not go so well. I once served him spaghetti with ketchup. (It was a red sauce, wasn't it?) and a frozen hamburger patty.

No, even though many times he tested my patience to the max, I didn't do it on purpose. What happened was that I took the patty out of the freezer and placed it under the broiler. Once it turned brown I thought it was cooked, so I put it on a plate together with an ear of corn that I had boiled for about five minutes and served it to him. When the poor kid tried to stick a fork in the hamburger, it struck the frozen center and just stood there, unable to penetrate the rest of the meat.

Eventually I learned how to put together a decent meal just in time for my mother's return, which couldn't have happened a moment sooner. I went back to the office and my brother went back to school properly fed, but we both learned to be a little more self-sufficient.

I never forgave my mother for leaving me and my brother alone in a strange country under those circumstances, but she always used to say: "your husband comes first."

I hope you are never put in a position where you have to choose between your husband or your children's needs. However, life has a way of playing tricks on us when we least expect it. Whatever you do, make sure you follow your heart.

And what if you are divorced or widowed, with children, and are starting a new relationship? Divorce is traumatic enough for kids, so please tread very carefully when introducing them to a new partner. Very young children will want to "adopt" any new man as their new daddy, particularly if theirs is no longer around due to death or abandonment. After my husband's untimely death, my young son would cozy up to any new man I dated, and it was heartbreaking to have to tell him that I was not going to marry them. Teenagers, on the other hand, will resist the idea of a new man in their mother's life.

If you were the one who left, you are faced with a double whammy. The divorce itself, which creates a rift in the family, not to mention a possible change in your standard of living, and the fact that they will tend to view their father as the victim and you as the evil doer.

Never mind that you were the sole breadwinner while he struggled to "find himself" for years, or that he followed every skirt in town, the fact that you wanted the divorce will mark you as the culprit in your children's eyes. Don't forget that all children want is to keep their family intact—and that is what they will dream about for years after you split up.

It is very important at this point to preserve the integrity of both parents in the eyes of the children. Whatever you tell them, even if they need to hear the truth, phrase it in a non-accusatory manner so they can understand the reason for the split without blaming any of the parties involved.

Therefore it is best to wait until a new relationship is firmly established before bringing your new beau to meet your kids. This is particularly important in the case of boys, who will tend to be overprotective of their mother.

Once the relationship is on a firm footing, your kids will benefit from seeing their mother happy once again and will be more inclined to accept a new man in their lives.

10

Keep the Mystery Going

Contrary to what they tell you, men love games. If that were not true, football, tennis, backgammon and poker wouldn't be such huge businesses. Men learn to play games as little children and games are part of their lives until they die.

You, or more precise, conquering you, is also part of a game. So why should you deny him the pleasure of discovering you, bit by bit, by opening up too soon? He doesn't have to know everything there is to know about you in one sitting. You have to open up slowly, like a flower, to keep him interested long enough so he can fall in love with you.

Remember our friend with the four children? She only let him meet two at a time! In *A Thousand and One Arabian Nights* Scheherazade, who is a smart girl if there ever was one, realizes that if she gives in too soon she will only be another harem girl. Instead she keeps the sultan under her spell by telling him one tale every night, and he, enthralled by Scheherazade's stories, keeps coming back for more.

Now mind you, all Scheherazade is doing with the sultan so far is talking, there is no hanky-panky of any kind. And this is a man who is used to getting what he wants, when he wants it. But our girl is hanging in there for a thousand and one nights! The more credit to her. By the time Scheherazade tells him her last story, the sultan is so smitten that he makes her his queen.

I'm not telling you to hold back for a thousand nights, and this is not a novel, it's your life. Neither him, nor you, if you really like him, want to wait that long, but keep the mystery going as far as you can. In the meantime, talk to him; enchant him with some of your life's experiences and your witty observations.

Men, like women, need some time to develop attachment and fondness. Sexual chemistry develops much quicker, especially for men, but you need both to fall in love. Time is on your side, so give your relationship time to develop by getting to know each other thoroughly before you take it to the sexual plane.

Should You Trust Him?

The short answer is a definite No.

Carolina was seeing a high-profile banker for four years. During that time he proposed several times and she declined, but kept seeing him. He was quite a bit older and she was comfortable just being his girlfriend, having three teenage daughters at home. "I would have to please too many people," she used to say, "him, me and my three daughters."

Then he was suddenly transferred to another town and the relationship started to deteriorate. Carolina didn't want to move to the small town where he was now living and told him that it was better to separate for a while. To her utter amazement, he agreed. This was a man who had taken her all over the country in his private jet and bought her $5,000 watches. But he was ready to let her go without a whimper. Now, Carolina is a smart girl and that got her thinking.

She didn't have to think too long. A week later she got a call from a friend. They had seen her banker at an airport with a young blonde. How long had this been brewing? Again the answer came quickly. The new woman found out about her, got a hold of her phone number and called her. It turned out the relationship had been going on for several years, with trips to his apartment in Florida, where Carolina lived (apparently when Carolina had been away on vacation with her daughters) as well as New York, where he kept a second home.

Needless to say Carolina was enraged. How come this woman had just found out about her? Hadn't she seen her pictures? They were all over his apartments. They had taken pictures during ski vacations with her daughters and in many of the social functions they attended together, and they were prominently displayed—but apparently not when *she* visited. He had had the presence of mind to hide them whenever the new woman was in either one of his homes.

The good part is that once the new woman found out about Carolina, she broke up with him as well. He learned a lesson, but so did Carolina. You don't leave a man alone for too long, and you don't trust him from here to the corner drugstore if he has the two most potent aphrodisiacs on earth: power and money.

Would things have been different had she agreed to marry him? Perhaps. But I believe that the time he spent alone had more to do with it than a wedding band. Men use absence as an opportunity. Perhaps my mother was right to go back to meet my father in Havana when he sent for her after all

11

Find Your Purpose

There is no surer way to capture the heart of an exciting man than to become an exciting woman. And there is nothing more conducive to living an exciting life than a sense of purpose. Having a purpose is like navigating life with the help of a compass: a purpose will always point you North, no matter where you happen to be.

Getting up in the morning with the itch to implement a new twist on a contract negotiation, or to mix a new color on a canvas is like manna from heaven for the soul. It fires up our neurons and places our whole body in a state of immediate alert. Suddenly everything we do is imbued with a new vitality, we feel and look young and energized. The Hindus call this *dharma*, or life's purpose, and they believe that each one of us has been granted a unique set of abilities that will allow us to realize this lifework. They also believe that it is the divine duty of each one of us to make good use of that ability in this lifetime.

In *The Monk that Sold his Ferrari* Robin Sharma tells the story of a yogi who was an excellent marksman. One day while walking through the forest he attached a rose to the trunk of a tree and then had his disciple cover his eyes with a handkerchief. After being blindfolded, he asked his pupil "How far from the rose am I?"

"One hundred feet," his pupil guessed.

"Have you ever observed me in my daily practice of this ancient art of archery?" the sage queried, knowing well the response that would come.

"I have seen you strike the bull's eye from a mark almost three hundred feet away and I cannot recall a time when you have ever missed at your current distance," the pupil answered.

Then with his eyes covered by the cloth and his feet placed securely on the ground, the teacher drew the bow with all his energy and released the arrow— aiming directly at the rose hanging from the tree. The arrow struck the large oak with a thud, missing its mark by an embarrassingly large distance.

"You will never be able to hit a target that you cannot see" was the yogi's lesson of the day. This is the most important principle for anyone seeking to attain his/ her goals and to fulfill his/her life's purpose. You have to set your goal before you can achieve it.

Fine, you may say. Finding your purpose is easy if you are born with an unusual talent, or a very clear idea of what you want to do. My brother, for instance, knew since he was a kid that he wanted to be a doctor and he set out in life with an unwavering target that he jumped through hoops to accomplish.

I still remember the day when he came home to the small apartment we used to rent in South Beach before South Beach became glamorous, and announced to my mother that he wanted to study medicine.

"How are we going to pay for school?" my mother asked, thinking of the meager budget we used to live on.

"Don't worry," he answered, "I'll find the way." And find it he did. He graduated with honors from Tulane University on loans and scholarships. That it took him the first four years of practice to pay them back is another story, but he became a doctor and never looked back.

I do believe that immigrants have a more pressing desire to succeed for the simple reason that they start with a disadvantage. They lack the comfort and backing of an established family and it is only up to them to get ahead. That may explain the success of the Cubans in Miami or the

Mexicans in California, but everyone can find a purpose and live a more fulfilling, focused life, whether they come from privilege of not, and having an established family to point the way, although it may eliminate the sense of urgency, can certainly smooth the ride. So go for it.

Your purpose may be to raise a wonderful family, help the poor or find the cure for cancer. Or you may have a way with people and decide to get in the political arena or start a public relations firm. You may have a beautiful singing voice or a way to produce beautiful images, either by painting or photography. The sky is the limit. Be relentless in the search for your *dharma*, we were all born with one.

If you happen to be born with an artistic bent you will be doubly blessed, for artists engage their sensual nature while implementing their craft. A sculptor models the pliable clay with her fingers, using her highly developed sense of touch to mold out of it beautiful figures; a composer brings together musical notes to craft an unforgettable melody by the mastery of her sense of hearing, and a painter recreates on her canvas the beauty of form and color that she absorbs with her heightened perception of the world around her. If you watch an artist at work you will notice her total concentration on the task at hand, for she is enraptured by what she's doing—and can't help but bring some of that heightened sense of being into her everyday existence to illuminate those around her.

I'll tell you something else. Once you zero in on your purpose, things will start coming to you as if by magic. There is a reason for this. The mind is like a big magnifying glass. Once it focuses on a subject, it will tend to eliminate all other distractions and will guide you to the fulfillment of your goals. Have you ever become interested in a subject, say a new designer or a new car and find that everywhere you go, you seem to find more of the same? That's a good example of the filtering power of your mind working overtime in the attainment of your goals.

And you don't necessarily have to hit it big to feel purposeful. The fact that I'm writing this book, without knowing if anyone else outside of my family and friends will ever take the time to read it is proof of what I'm saying. All new writers start that way, and one in a million gets published.

Does that thought ever deter me from my goal? Not at all. I have as strong a need to write down my thoughts as an athlete has to run a triathlon. If you find yourself reading this, it will mean that I got published and hopefully both you and I will be happy.

But every morning when I wake up I can't wait to get to my laptop to put down in writing the thoughts that have been flying around my mind the previous day, even as I do my morning walk on the treadmill. Writing this book has given me a wonderful sense of purpose and excitement at an unusually stressful time in my life.

So go ahead and find yours. We all have one, whether you were born in Wichita, Singapore or Mexico City, the world is waiting for your contribution. Go out there and shine and don't worry about the outcome. If you are excited enough about what you do, the world will take notice, and even if you don't become a household name, the process will energize your life to a degree you have never experienced before.

Fine, you may say, that is all good, but I'm not sixteen any more with the whole world waiting for me to turn into a success.

Can I tell you a secret? Many women have found their purpose relatively late in life, after raising families, losing a mate to death or divorce or simply when they have found themselves with nothing of value to do with their time. Jacqueline Kennedy Onassis became an editor at Doubleday after losing her famous husband to an assassin and her stature as First Lady. Indira Ghandi didn't become Prime Minister of India until the death of her iconic husband, and thousands of other unknown women have found purpose starting new careers after raising their children.

Years ago I was contemplating going to law school. I was then in my forties and worried that by the time I graduated I was going to be fifty. I was discussing this dilemma with a trusted older friend. She looked me in the eye, cocked her head and said: "You know something, Betty, in four years you are going to be fifty, whether or not you go to law school. So you might as well go for it." As it turns out, I did not go to law school, turned fifty and beyond and here I am writing this book, which I find is my real passion.

It is no coincidence that purpose and passion start with the same letter. One always ushers in the other, and there is nothing more attractive to a man, or anyone for that matter, than a passionate woman. Once you start living your life in this manner, passion will permeate every aspect of your new, exhilarating existence, so watch out for the consequences... you may be in for a fun ride.

Go Where Your Passion Takes You

Hopefully by now you have given some serious thoughts to the ways in which you can find your passion. Let me give you an example of what can happen to your life once you do. Olga Connor is a good friend of mine. She is also an excellent journalist with a weekly entertainment column in Miami's *El Nuevo Herald* and a woman of passion.

Whatever Olga undertakes she doesn't do halfway, whether it is organizing a cultural trip to a remote region of the planet or writing a book, Olga is all there. She is one of those people that looks as if she is about to do something mischievous and wonderful whenever you see her, but is not about to tell you; and has that rare gift that only totally engaged people have of raising the energy level of those around her by just being in her presence.

"I believe that you should be in the places that make you happy, doing the things that trigger your passion," she tells me with her perennial grin, hazel eyes sparkling with recollection.

"Thirty years ago I was attending a poetry reading in Philadelphia, where I was going to college," adds Olga—who ever since I've known her has been unapologetically "pleasantly plump."

"I had, even then, a few extra pounds, but when I walked into that room I could sense the eyes of every man resting on me. I was particularly excited about the reading, and full of happiness after some serious soul searching that brought on an unexpected cultural enlightenment, and it must have reflected in my face. I guess you could say I was experiencing a cultural high that illuminated my whole being. Thinking about it now, I must have been a real magnet at that moment, and boy did I attract the energy in that room!"

Energy is a measurable force, some of which emanates from human beings. It is only recently through the findings of Quantum Physics that science has come to corroborate what mystics, from cabbalists to yogis, have been preaching for centuries. Our thoughts turn into feelings, and feelings have power and a certain vibrational frequency that attracts like-minded energies. A woman who is full of purpose and passion is going to create a magnetic attraction into her field of energy without even trying. She will do so by the sheer power of her feelings, while she is engaged in the creation of the life she wants.

So go ahead and put your heart and soul into everything you do. Listen to the music and move with passion when you're dancing... sing to the top of your lungs... pour your feelings into a novel... express all your creativity in a painting... take that Mediterranean cruise you've been dreaming about—concentrate on what really turns you on and leave the rest to the universe.

It doesn't hurt either that doing the things you enjoy, whether it is traveling, bowling, playing tennis or collecting antiques, you are going to meet people who will be compatible with you for the simple reason that they share the same interests. That's why unless you are a drinker, it is not a good idea to go to bars. Think of who you are going to meet in there: other drinkers.

I always know when my friend, the tango dancer, is coming back from a tango session. Her cheeks are flushed and there is a twinkle in her eyes and a new spring in her step. I have come to accept that when I see her looking that way, I'm not to ask too many questions. All I know is that she has just had a wonderful time. "An hour of hugs," as she playfully puts it.

Life is short. Whenever possible, be where you want to be and do the things you like to do, chances are you will be so excited about what you are doing at that moment that something wonderful is going to happen.

12

Eight Ways to Secure your Relationship

Be Sweet

"You catch more flies with honey than with vinegar,"* my mother used to tell me whenever she saw me about to get into a flight of anger at my boyfriend. The Latin culture encourages women to be sweet, and Latin women tend to easily express their affection, particularly for the men in their lives—if I may say, with exceptionally good results.

Suppose you want to see a particular movie that you know will not be to your man's liking. Instead of getting into an ugly argument, the Latin woman will stroke her man's hand, look into his eyes and sweetly murmur: *"Mi amor,* me llevas a ver *Sex and the City* esta noche? *me muero por verla, papito!"* "My love, will you take me to see *Sex and the City* tonight? I'm dying to see it daddy!"

Papito which translates into "daddy" is one of the ultimate terms of endearment in Spanish, not to be confused with "sugar daddy", which has a completely different connotation in English. You can bet your man would rather stay home and watch a Dolphins game or else go see an action movie, but how could he refuse you when you ask so sweetly?

Chances are you'll get to see your movie, which may even inspire an evening of passionate love making.

Latins are big on terms of endearment. In fact, there is a whole vocabulary that is used generously between lovers, such as *mi cielo, mi vida, gordito, mi bombon, mi corazon, mi preciosura, mi amor, cariñito, amor de mi vida*... These are just the ones that come to mind. However, the Latin woman does not restrict the use of these superlatives to the man in her life, *au contraire*. She generously offers them to her children, her relatives and any friends that elicit her affection. She has no inhibitions showing her love for anyone that she feels close to. When Latins meet each other it is *de rigueur* to kiss on the cheek, whether it is a man or a woman, and if you watch people at a cocktail party, Latins tend to stand close to one another. A peck on the cheek to the host and hostess is also expected before leaving a reception, as well as to whoever happens to be standing nearby.

We crave affection and our women are not ashamed to show it. If you watch a group of Latin women at a luncheon you will see that they are leaning towards each other, and not only to catch the latest gossip; we truly seek that human warmth that emanates from friends that we have usually kept through a lifetime.

This, by the way is something else that differentiates us. In our countries friendships are kept forever. Being that America is such a big country, people tend to move around and create new friendships wherever they go, many times short-lived. In Latin countries people live all their lives in one place, and friends stay close to one another to help, reminisce and just enjoy a big social circle. In my case, when I emigrated from Cuba so did all my friends and many of them stayed in Miami. When I tell my American friends that I have lunch once a month with girlfriends I know since kindergarten they are pleasantly surprised. We're really there for one another!

Show your vulnerability

Believe it or not, even in these liberated times, men are hardwired to protect their women; it goes back to that hunter instinct, and a woman who is not afraid to show her vulnerable side will have an easier ride with her man. Sheltering you from harm makes him feel powerful and manly, which is in tune with his masculinity and sense of well being. "Not that you should act helpless, but letting him see your vulnerable side will bring him closer because it unlocks his instincts to take care of you," says David Givens, PhD, author of *Love Signals*. A Latin woman is well aware of this and often gives her man little jobs to show his prowess in a man's field. Fixing a leaky faucet or figuring out how to get rid of the bugs in your computer, the fact that he can prove his ability to help you, will make him feel ten feet tall when he's around you. But make sure you thank him afterwards… and refer to his success in front of others if you want extra points. Ask his opinion about your 401K or your new lease, it will show that you value the way he thinks… and you may end up with a few good pointers to boot.

These are all ways to validate him. What else? Wear whatever he gives you, whether a new perfume or a new watch. It will show not only that you enjoy and appreciate his gift, but also that you value him over any other man that might have been in your life.

Make him feel at ease about your relationship

One of single men's biggest fears is to become lost when they become half of a couple. If you can keep your desire to change him in check, you will be halfway into ushering your man into what he will perceive as an easy, comfortable fit. Men feel, often with good reason, that women will chip away at their identity until they become totally domesticated and, in their eyes, castrated, when they get into a serious relationship. By making it clear that you don't expect your man to change, he'll feel that you truly understand him and don't threaten his sense of self.

Trust me, once he has relaxed into an easy relationship with you, you can start the process of adapting him to your life using the sweetness that we discussed before. The key is to do this slowly and sweetly. In the end he will feel so comfortable with you that he will begin to see his changes as something positive instead of threatening, and he may even wonder how he could have lived the way he did before he met you!

Share With Him Your Own Fear of Commitment

Men often see women as hungry ring-hunters when they just want to have fun. If you are afraid to commit, share your concerns with your man and let him know you are in this together, navigating the same choppy waters instead of trying to trap him. This goes hand in hand with what we discussed before. A Latin woman enjoys the ride as much as the end result, and often gets the man she wants for that very same reason. Remember, his need to protect himself is gone once he relaxes into an easy, comfortable relationship in which he is having as much fun as you are.

Our friend Serena celebrated her attorney's decision to stay single, and in so doing she placed herself in the same camp, becoming a comrade in arms so to speak, and planting the seeds for the beginning of their friendship. But more importantly, she set herself apart from all the other women he had dated. She had become unique in his eyes.

Keep Him Fascinated with Different Aspects of You

One of men's biggest fears when entering a serious relationship is that of becoming bored by being always with the same woman. Man is genetically programmed to impregnate as many females as he can and therefore to seek variety in his love life. Your challenge then, if you want to keep him happy, is to reinvent yourself every once in while and show him different facets of you. By doing so you will make him feel like he is always with a new person without having to stray.

This applies to your appearance as well as your personality. Wear your hair up one day with pale lip color and heavier than usual eye makeup. Down in fashionable waves or straight down your back with red lips and lip gloss for a Hollywood starlet look another day. And while we're in the subject of makeup, if he's early for a date, instead of letting him wait in the living room, let him see you putting on lipstick and powdering your nose. This is a very intimate ritual for a woman and the fact that you let him share it with you enhances your sense of trust.

Sometimes you may have to resort to more drastic measures to keep him interested. Remember, all's fair in love and war. Teresa, a lively Chilean journalist confided that she once performed a strip tease in order to get the attention of her American husband, whom she met and married in Chile.

"He was acting too *American*" she told me with a chuckle, "you know, only thinking about work, and I missed the passion and the frisky lovemaking of our first years together, when he was more preoccupied with which wine to have with dinner than with the company bottom line. I have to tell you, my performance really got his attention!"

Read up on current affairs to keep him interested and enjoy a lively discussion every once in a while. Get immersed in a new hobby, like jewelry making and show him the results of your craft, or take dancing lessons and mesmerize him by teaching him your new salsa moves. In short, make him feel like he is courting a different woman every few months and you will keep him content and happy as a clam for years to come.

"She never bored me," confided a widower who after forty years of marriage still mourns the loss of the love of his life. I don't know about you, but that's how I would like to be remembered.

Respect His Privacy

Even in the closest of relationships, there are boundaries we need to respect, and crossing over them can lead to real problems when there is really no need for it. For instance, many men keep an office at home. Treat that as his sacred space and stay out of it, other than to straighten it out every once in a while—if he asks you to.

One of the worst arguments I ever had with my husband had to do with my efforts to tidy up his space. We had ordered a new desk for his home office and having asked him to no avail to clean up the pile of papers on his old one in preparation for the new arrival, I decided to take matters into my own hands. When the new desk came in, I took all his papers, rearranged them in neat little piles and eagerly awaited his delighted comments.

"What have you done? He exclaimed the minute he got home. "I can't find anything!" The fact was that he knew where everything was in his own disorder, and I vowed never again to intrude, to the delight of both of us.

Let Him in the Kitchen

Latin women cook for their men, but if he is a gourmand, or even if he just likes the smell of what you're cooking, it's a good idea to let him help you every once in a while. We can't emphasize enough the relationship between food and love. Remember, the first sign of nurturing he received from his mother was when she fed him. Not that you want him to think of you as such, God forbid, but food and love are intricately entwined. In fact it has been demonstrated that being around food increases the levels of oxytocin, the attachment hormone, in males.

The more often he shares food experiences with you, the more he will associate you with the good feelings he derives from it. So go food shopping together, visit farmers markets, make food an integral part of your relationship and see it flourish. You will also get a good idea of his food choices so that you can prepare his favorite dishes later on.

By the same token it is advisable to introduce food talk early on in a relationship. Discuss with him what you're cooking for dinner and what you love to eat. Tell him which are your favorite restaurants and watch his reaction. If you like healthy food and he is a meat and potatoes man or a junk food addict, you will know this is not a match made in heaven.

But not to worry, all's not lost. You may decide to give the relationship a chance and introduce him to the way you eat, but again, do this slowly. Say things like: "There's a new Thai-sushi place that I'm dying to try. How about going there tonight!" Once there, order the cucumber-wrapped rolls that you love and let him try one; he may find out that he likes it. Introduce him to steamed edamame; these salted soybeans are fun to snack on and have all the benefits of soy in a neat little package…he may catch on. After a few of these culinary adventures you can cook dinner and serve your tilapia with sun-dried tomato sauce, but don't tell him yet that you used whipped tofu instead of cream for the sauce. It takes a while to adapt psychologically to this kind of eating, but he may. Who knows, perhaps the poor darling simply didn't have someone to cook healthy for him before.

Once the relationship advances, stock your pantry with the brands of products you know he likes; he will begin to feel at home at your place, and it won't hurt if you let him take a nap in your sofa for added comfort, or if you fall asleep in his arms while you're watching TV. These are samples of domesticity that he will begin to appreciate without you having to argue the point. When he is so comfortable with you that he stops thinking about the *relationship* and simply enjoys it, is when he will start falling in love with you.

Don't Be a Yes Woman

You don't have to see eye to eye on everything. A Latin woman will be sweet and gentle, but she will never lose her essence. By that I mean that we maintain our core beliefs intact, even after entering into a relationship with a man. The image of the submissive Latin woman is not quite accurate. More often than not what you will see is a woman who is not afraid to voice her own opinions. It is important to show that you have a backbone and are not afraid to speak your mind. Your man will definitely respect you for that. What you have to remember is to voice those opinions in a manner that is respectful of his own and, most importantly, does not belittle him.

You may agree with him on most subjects, which may very well be the case, but if you're passionate about something, show it. The more you stick to your essence, the more of your individuality will show and the more interesting you will be to others. The intellectual challenge of a good thought-out argument never fails to provide a welcome spark to a waning relationship. If a man is married to a woman who agrees with him on everything, after a while she will become no more than an echo of himself. He will end up feeling alone... and will begin to look for company.

13

Find a Man Who "Gets" You

There's an old Spanish saying: *man is like a bear, the uglier the more attractive*. I wouldn't go that far, but in choosing a mate, you will be better advised to look for an intangible that I have always found more important.

There are men who would be considered unattractive by less discriminating women than I, and who I have found irresistible. Yes, I know, this is a confusing statement. I used the word discriminating because there is a quality that I pick up in a man right away and it has nothing to do with his looks.

I'm referring to an affinity of purpose, a shared need that comes through, at least for me, loud and clear, making me feel that we're co-conspirators, fellow travelers on this wonderful journey that we call life. It has to do with the way he moves, the way he establishes eye contact and the depth of his thinking. Ah! Here we get to the important part. The way a man thinks, his quickness of mind, his wit, for me is a much greater turn on than a well-developed pair of deltoids or a perfect nose.

If a man "gets" me, if I can tell him a funny story and he can laugh with me, if he picks up right away on my innuendos, we're on the same wavelength and it's sheer joy.

There are men who walk around with a twinkle in their eyes that lets the world know they are having a wonderful time by just being on the planet. And if I can contribute to that twinkle, if I can light up those eyes, I'm in heaven, no matter what color they happen to be. If I can make him laugh during the first ten minutes of conversation, it's almost a done deal.

There's no bigger turn off than a man with a deficient sense of humor. That alone, at least for me, is an Olympic-sized joy killer, no matter what else is happening in the relationship. Even the most luxurious surroundings fail to cushion the blow that such a dead end to happiness and spontaneity can bring. Just to give you an example, whenever I used to tell a joke to my ex-husband, would you believe that I had to back up and explain the punch line? It was exhausting!

I believe that it takes intelligence and wit to see humor in every-day situations. Every human condition, from marital relations to rearing children and growing old has a joke to go with it, and being able to laugh at it and see the irony of it all makes life more bearable. It makes husband and wife partners in crime so to speak, simply because being able to take in stride whatever life dishes out, cements the bonding of a good relationship. Humor and intelligence go hand in hand. And intelligence, the way I see it, is the ultimate aphrodisiac.

So promise me from now on that the next time you meet a man you will test his sense of humor. If he laughs with you, if he "gets" you, forget his bald spot and get him some Rogaine. At least a bald spot is fixable. A flat personality is not.

14

Is There a Prince Out There?

Should You Stay Home While You Wait for Yours?

The answer is a definite no. You need to keep flexing your relationship muscles. Remember that anything you don't use, you lose. Have you ever seen the expression in the face of some of your friends that have sworn off men? The sole mention of the word elicits a contraction of lips and a rigidity of body and mind that broadcast to the world they have closed up shop. You don't want that to happen to you. I am a firm believer that, as long as a girl is single, she should have men friends to keep her in the game. By that I don't mean that you should be intimate with men you are not ready to commit to, but you can have admirers for going to a play, to take to a social event and just to chat with and display your womanly charms to. After all, practice makes perfect and you don't want —God forbid—your juices to dry up.

Is it dishonest to pal around with an admirer you don't intend to have a relationship with? Not as long as you are sincere with him from the very beginning and explain that all you want is a friendship. At that point it is up to him to accept the rules of the game or to decline and go hunting some place else. I'm a firm believer that as long as a girl is unattached, she should have different men friends. One may be a fabulous dancer, another may have a brilliant mind, another one may play a mean game of tennis, and still another one may be a good confidant. Until you have the one that satisfies your soul, it is fine to keep several male friends around you. After all, it is the interaction with the opposite sex that keeps you feeling like a woman.

I don't need to tell you that you should treasure your girlfriends. I have never canceled plans with a girlfriend because a man asked me out. Girlfriends will always be there whether or not there's a man in your life and will offer company and support no matter what's happening. Nurture your friendship with women. But men friends, even though platonic, will always remind you that you are a *woman*.

But, you may ask, what about them? Aren't you wasting their time? What do they get out of their relationship with you if there is no intimacy?

The pleasure of your company. Yes, never underestimate what a woman like you can bring to a man's life, which is essentially what they are bringing to yours: camaraderie, spice and good times spent with the opposite sex. And don't even mention to me that what I'm suggesting is a waste of time for the two of you. That sounds like your mother talking. Remember, you are a charming, modern woman and time goes by whether you are enjoying it or not. I say, make the most out of every moment until your prince arrives…you never know how long it will take.

Should You Hold Out for Perfection?

That question reminds me of an epiphany I had many years ago during a visit to Japan. We were touring one of the famous gardens the Japanese are well known for. Every inch of space was lovingly detailed, with sculptures and lanterns accentuating perfectly trimmed hedges and bonsai, the miniature trees which they prune until their roots stop growing, in order to fit the space allotted to them. Small ponds were filled with colorful trout which sparkled in the sun like submerged jewels and came up to catch the food that our group kept throwing at them. When we finished touring the garden, to my surprise, and that of the other people in the tour, we came to a corner that was left unfinished. It just stood out like a sore thumb in the middle of all that lovely greenery, completely bare.

"Why is that corner empty?" I asked the guide, intrigued by the obvious oversight, "are they still working on the garden?"

"No," she answered with a big grin, "the garden is finished."

"So why," I insisted, "is that corner empty?"

This time the guide smiled openly, and turning to me, loud enough for the whole group to hear, exclaimed: "That corner was left bare on purpose, to remind us that we have to learn to love imperfection."

I never forgot that and many years later I am telling you that you will never find a perfect man. If you are holding out for someone who will be handsome, bright and successful, caring, sensitive and a good dancer, I am telling you that you may be in for a very long wait. Men who are very successful often get there by stepping on other people's toes and you can't expect them to be sensitive and caring, at least not until they finish the climb to wherever it is they want to go. A very good looking man may have two left feet and so on. But what you should definitely hold out for is the man who is perfect for *you*. The one who fits your particular needs and quirks, which may not be your sister's, your mother's or your best friend's.

He may not be handsome, and may even sport a pot belly, but he may just know how to tickle your funny bone, and be sensuous and brilliant. Or he may be extremely successful and you admire him above all men because he brings you into another world, filled with possibilities and interesting people. And let's not forget the power a man like this wields, which for many women is the ultimate aphrodisiac.

Whatever your requirements are, there will be someone who will fulfill them, and that is non-negotiable. Even if your sister, your mother or your best friend do not find him attractive, if he's attractive to you, that is the perfection you should hold out for. Remember that for every pot there's a cover, meaning the fit has to be there, for that is what in the end will make you happy. Being with the right man will also allow you to withstand the ups and downs that life invariably brings in a much better fashion, for being with the right partner will always cushion the blows. I don't know about you, but for me everything looks rosier in the morning if I wake up with a strong pair of arms that have been holding me tight through the night, wrapped around me.

15

A Latin Southern Belle and Other Stories

When Marta met Gene they were both vacationing at the old Saxony Hotel in Miami Beach. "He was much older than me. I was just nineteen and he was already thirty one. What drew him to me believe or not, was a Jewish star," she tells me, her smile lighting up her face, framed by thick salt and pepper hair, cut stylishly short.

"There we were my parents and I yakking away in Spanish in the lobby of the Saxony. The fact that I was wearing a Jewish star seemed incongruous with my language and one of the young men that was sitting nearby got up to call Gene to tell him about us. He came over and asked where we were from. When we told him we were from Havana, he asked why we were wearing a Jewish star. 'Why shouldn't we wear one, 'I replied, 'we're Jewish!'

At that point, totally confused, but charmed, he asked me out."

Remember the story about the chaperone? Well, Marta's father was a bit more lenient. He only insisted that they had to double date, and Gene obliged, asking his friend to come along with a date. Marta and Gene corresponded for a year and the following summer, at the same hotel, he asked her to marry him, but the marriage wouldn't take place, at her father's insistence, until she turned twenty, which was a year later.

What was it like for a Cuban woman living in North Carolina in the 1950's?

"I was young, much younger than all the other girls in our crowd and oh so polite and naïve! They all fell in love with me," says Marta. "Thank God this was the South, I can't imagine how I would have fared had Gene lived in New York instead! Even in the 50's, when I got married, I was much more submissive and accommodating than the other girls. None of us worked, but I was coming from a family where my father ruled and my mother followed. I was taught to be charming and accepting of all circumstances."

Marta learned to love Gastonia, the small town where she settled with Gene in North Carolina. They had three children, she learned to play tennis and host beautiful parties, like a proper Southern woman, but her Latin roots beckoned and eventually, after her family started a thriving shoe business in South Florida, they moved to Miami. Shortly after she and Gene opened a travel agency which they ran together right up to Gene's death, which happened on a cruise ship, in the middle of the ocean.

Marta ran the travel agency alone for a while, but eventually sold it and worked at another agency for a couple of years until she retired. She has been happily involved in a relationship for the last fifteen years, but doesn't want to get married again.

"I've become quite a bit more assertive. I don't believe another marriage is in the cards for me. I like things the way they are now. But if I were to think back, I truly believe that what charmed Gene fifty years ago in the lobby of the Saxony Hotel was the fact that I was so different from all the other girls he knew."

Let the Rhythm Get You

We talked before about the power of dancing. Sometimes dancing is just the right ingredient to break the ice and bring two people together that might otherwise never have been a pair.

For some men, particularly those who are not very verbal, music offers a welcome avenue to express hidden feelings, and a woman who can relate to this type of man through music will be able to understand in his own dancing "shorthand" what otherwise would be impossible to read.

My friend Marisa was vacationing in San Juan while combining a bit of business when she received a call from the big hotel chain she worked for in New York asking her to visit an important client in St. Thomas. That same day she took an afternoon flight to the island and, after her meeting was over, came up to the bar of the hotel with one of the executives for a night cap. She finished her drink and was about to leave when her client introduced her to a good looking young man who was sitting at the bar with his father nursing a Margarita.

"The minute we were introduced he said hello, turned around and unceremoniously went back to his drink," she told me forty years later as we sipped cappuccinos at a trendy Bal Harbour café across from the oceanfront apartment building where she lives, one sunny summer afternoon not too long ago. "His father, on the other hand, fell in love with me on the spot and we kept talking for quite a while."

Marisa wasn't back in her room for more than fifteen minutes when the phone rang. It was Leonard apologizing for his rudeness. "I'm sure his father bowled him out," she says laughing, the fiery red hair that she used to wear long and wild now smartly coiffed in a short bob.

"He asked me out to dinner the following night, and he had planned to show me the old St. Thomas Synagogue, reputably the oldest in the Western Hemisphere.

Needless to say we never made it to the synagogue. After dinner he took me dancing to a night club frequented by the local people of the island and that was when we really hit it off. As soon as the music started, out went all his inhibitions. To my utter amazement, this man had rhythm… and, being Cuban, that made me look at him in a completely different manner. As shy and reticent as he had been before, all his feelings came out on that dance floor. What can I tell you, he danced like a Latin man!"

Marisa was going back to San Juan the following morning, but when her flight was called she looked up from her seat, ticket in hand, and there was Leonard at the airport begging her to stay. Needless to say she canceled the flight and left the following day, but not before getting his graduation ring and promising not to date anyone else in New York.

Have a Life Besides the One You Share with Him

"I believe that what charmed my husband when I first met him was my innocence," says Rita, one of my childhood friends who met her husband when she was eighteen and him close to thirty. However, unbeknown to her she had already made quite an impression. "He remembered the color of each one of the bathing suits I used to wear at our beach club," she tells me with a chuckle. Married more than forty years, Rita confides that the secret to her very happy long-standing marriage is a combination of a good sense of humor and great communication. And the fact that they always have set aside time to be alone together.

Even when her husband, an international businessman, traveled for two or three weeks at a time, she would leave her four children with her mother and meet him, whether he was in the Orient or the Caribbean. "I always knew who the captain of my ship was," she tells me without hesitation. "I knew I couldn't leave him alone for such a long time. Whenever a man travels there are temptations. There are women everywhere, and Rodolfo talks even to stones if there's no one else around. I wasn't going to take that chance!"

To keep a sense of intimacy in the middle of a growing family, Rita and Rodolfo used to plan trips to a nearby beach resort, and disappear for a few days, just the two of them. "We didn't tell anyone, we would just pack up and leave."

And now that the children are gone? "We give each other lots of space," she tells me. "Rodolfo is retired, but he keeps an office downtown where he goes every day to work on his philanthropic projects, and has lunch with interesting friends. I'm busy with my children and grand-children—as well as my girlfriends."

American society revolves around couples and very often men and women do everything together, particularly after retirement. The ads for retirement communities show men and women happily playing golf or ten-nis together—the dream being that they will live happily like this ever after.

Latin women know that no man or woman can satisfy all of our needs. Having other people to interact with, and individual experiences that can be shared with a spouse at the end of the day keeps a marriage vital and refreshed, even after retirement.

The Latin culture encourages having separate friends as well as common friends who come in and out of our lives at different times and help us keep our sense of identity, and perhaps a little mystery, outside of the couple. The fact that we can keep surprising our partner by sharing our individual experiences over the years instead of spending every waking moment with him is an insurance against boredom and familiarity. These two things, if left unchecked, will eventually erode the vitality of even the best of marriages.

If you're single, having a life of your own is a given, but many women make the mistake of immediately wrapping their lives around their new love once they're interested in a man, when just the opposite is what will usually clinch the deal. Knowing that you're busy with your own social life —which more often than not at this point will consist of going out with your girlfriends, even though he doesn't have to know that—will make you more desirable in his eyes.

Knowing that he has to wait his turn to take you out and you're not about to cancel plans because of him will also put an additional value on the pleasure of your company.

We Still Believe in Love... at Any Age.

Maria Isabel lost her husband at the ripe old age of seventy five. Being an extremely active woman all her life, she sold her business in San Juan and moved to Miami, where she joined an elder care charity.

In no time at all she became president of the association and went abroad with a group of other members. Being a vivacious Latin woman she caught the eye of a widower and embarked in a whirlwind romance that culminated in a very happy second marriage.

She had three children of her own and he had none. And even though this was a late second marriage for both, her friends arranged a well attended bridal shower where carefully wrapped favors were being passed around. "I feel like I'm twenty all over again," she told me, dark curls artfully arranged around her beaming face the day of the shower. "He wants to be with me all the time and calls me at all hours when we're not together. I've never had such an ardent lover."

There were several hundred guests at the wedding with a professional photographer and a formal wedding cake. And indeed she was as excited as a twenty-year old. Bridal shower, wedding and honeymoon proceeded as planned and the newlyweds moved into her apartment, which they later sold after he also sold his to buy a bigger one. Being that both are socially active, I run into them a lot, and whenever I do, would you believe that seven years later they are still holding hands?

Is Maria Isabel free of cares? Not in a million years! She has to help one of her children who has a heart ailment, but what this woman is and always was is a perennial optimist who gets a kick out of life. If I want to catch her early I have to call her before her aerobics class, which starts at eight. From then on she's out on errands and meetings all day long.

Love *can* come knocking at any age, if we just keep our ears trained to the ground, our spirits uplifted and our lives on track.

16

Less is More

When it comes down to it, a lot of what makes a Latin woman so different and alluring may have more to do with what she doesn't do than with what she does.

She doesn't take sex lightly, therefore she treads very cautiously when entering a new relationship. "Many women today are all for equality, including how they view their roles in relation to men's in a sexual relationship," says Stephanie, a Mexican-born publicist living in Miami. "Latin women as a whole come from much more conservative upbringings and we view sex as part of an emotional commitment."

She doesn't stand on ceremony. If someone wants to drop in for a visit, it's not unusual to just ring the bell or make last-minute plans on the run. "We are spontaneous creatures," says Stephanie.

She doesn't speak only one language. We are also worldly. It is not unusual for a Latin woman to speak several languages—a minimum of two, by definition.

She doesn't kiss and tell. For Latin women a relationship is something private that needs to be kept under wraps until it becomes serious. Discretion is a big part of how we conduct our private lives. If you ever watched a Telenovela (Spanish language soap operas that have become popular all over the world) you will see that the heroine always has a big secret lurking in her past that she is trying to keep secret at all costs.

She doesn't fit the mold. Being different has its own rewards, perhaps unfairly so. When Stephanie listed her profile in one of the most popular internet dating sites as "Sxy Latin" (the site did not allow the use of the world "sex" in any variation) she got, according to her tally, 300 responses! The word "Latin" did set her apart.

She doesn't reveal everything about herself in one sitting. A Latin woman tends to appear mysterious at first. Remember, we have a different background that in and of itself presents an enigma to an American or European man. A smart Latin woman will capitalize on this to keep her man interested. If you are different, a man will want to get to know you, partly out of curiosity, partly because he is intrigued by you and your past. But you don't have to be a Latin woman to create your own mystery. All you have to do is be somewhat reticent.

If a man asks a direct question, give him a vague answer. You never lie, just don't disclose everything...keep him guessing and he'll come back for more. One of the most consistent things that Latin women tell me when I ask them what attracted their man is "the fact that I was different." So create your own differences.

If you studied drama, emphasize your theatrical ability. If you were a great athlete, tell him about the time you won the tennis tournament. If you travel the world, let him know that you have been abroad, but keep it short. "Yes, it was all wonderful, but that was then and this is now, I'll tell you more about it some other time." Don't make it seem all important or life consuming... he is.

Life is About Experiences. Don't Be a Material Girl

When you get down to it, it is really what you feel and do that makes you happy, not what you have. A new car or a bigger house are dandy, but how long does it take before you get so used to them that you start taking them for granted?

A family dinner where everybody gets together, an outing with good friends is what we end up remembering as the good times. And very often very successful people miss the times when they were still struggling and see them as the most genuine period of their lives. These are some of the all-important things that will always warm up your heart:

A strong pair of arms holding you at night.

Potluck dinners with trusted friends.

Big family reunions to remind you where you came from.

Someone you're crazy about calling you "baby". I melt at that one!

The light in your man's eyes when you're all dressed up for a party.

Hearing him say you're the most beautiful woman in the room. Even if it's not true.

Making him proud of your accomplishments. Whether it's cooking a gourmet dinner, balancing your checkbook or writing the great American novel.

Holding your first baby together.

Being nice to your mother.

Being nice to your mother's friends.

Knowing that he fits in with your family. If he's going to share your life, both of you will be a lot happier if it's a good fit.

Listening to your worries when you can't sleep at night.

Kissing you first thing in the morning. Yes, even before you had a chance to brush your teeth. But make that one a peck, please...

Waking up before you to make coffee.

Getting you a perfect gift for your birthday. It doesn't need to be expensive, but just what you really wanted. (It means he's paying attention.)

Offering to give you a wake up call in the morning, even if he's in a different time zone where it's three hours earlier. That one really happened to me!

Covering you up at night when it's cold and you're too lazy to get up and get the blanket.

Offering his arm when you're stepping down at the movies and it's dark.

Offerng to do the dishes, even when it's not his turn.

There are countless ways in which a good man can make you happy. Caviar, champagne and diamonds would be a welcome part of your life--they're just wonderful things to have. But even if they're not, having a warm, wonderful human being by your side for the rest of your life can certainly smooth the ride. I hope that is the kind you will look for--and keep.

Honesty will take you far.

"I find Latin women more up front," says Ken, an American man who has dated several Latin women after his divorce. "They don't tell you that they're busy when you call them for a date if they're not, or that you should call them earlier in the week to make plans. If they want to go out with you, they say so. They don't play games, and I like that."

Ken recently went out with a Colombian lady he had met on an Internet site. "When we finally arranged a first date, after about an hour of conversation it was evident that we were not a match," he says. "I'm into sports big time and she has an artistic nature. I ordered mussels and a salad at the same time and the mussels were getting cold as we ate the salad, which she, a true gourmand, was quick to point out. I guess I struck out. But not completely.

She called me the following morning and said: 'Ken, you and I are not a match made in heaven, but you're a tennis player, would you like to meet a friend of mine who loves to play?' I liked the fact that she didn't lead me on, and that she thought enough of me to want to introduce me to a friend. I found that very thoughtful." A Latin woman will not be shy to tell a man she likes him if she does, and she will let him know in no uncertain terms if that happens to be the case. Or, as in Ken's case, she will let him down easy and find a way to turn things around in a positive way. Subtlety and diplomacy are also some of our traits. We really hate to be rude, and there's really no need for it. A charming sense of civility is part and parcel of the Latin culture.

Feelings

We are big on expressing feelings; our whole culture is based on that. If you listen to Latin songs, expressions of love are loud and clear. When you listen to the words of a tango, you can feel the pain of lost love and the longing for the loved one. And boleros are unabashedly romantic.

When Carlos Gardel sang *"El dia que me quieras"* (The day you love me) he sang about roses blooming, bells ringing and birds flying all at once just because his true love loved him back. Talk about intensity! We don't just fall in love, we swoon. Just like in our love songs, in our poetry there is drama in every word.

One of my favorite love poems belongs to the Chilean poet Pablo Neruda. In it he depicts the sensuality of love's longing with words that resemble paint brushes; such is the colorful expression of his thoughts:

"If I look at the crystal moon,
at the red branches
of the slow autumn at my window
If I touch near the fire
the impalpable ash
of the wrinkled body of the log
Everything carries me to you.
As if everything that exists:
aromas, light, metals
were little boats that sail
towards those isles of yours
that wait for me."

"Those isles of yours that wait for me." I can't think of a more poetic way to refer to the essence of a woman.

17

Passion is Our Second Name

Passion is what we're all about; we thrive on it and are not shy about expressing our passionate feelings.

"When a Latin woman kisses you, her whole heart is in that kiss," says Dave, another American man enamored of Latin women. "Many women kiss almost by rote, it's like they're doing homework," he says, "a Latin woman, on the other hand, gets really into it." As a matter of fact, there is a famous Spanish song called "El Beso," (The Kiss), and the words: "when a Spanish woman kisses, she really kisses" illustrate this point.

That goes back to the fact that we enjoy the whole process, not only the end result The marriage, the house, the children, will come later, but Latin girls are passionate creatures who put their heart and soul into every encounter when they love a man. They are also uninhibited. "There is nothing off limits to a Latin woman," says Dave. "They are very giving lovers and the fact that they enjoy the process, makes everything seem natural and whole.

There is one thing that comes with the passion, though," he adds, with a glint in his eye. "They can be extremely jealous. Maybe because in the Latin culture it is not unusual for men—whether they are married or not—to cheat, they overreact in situations because they don't trust their man to be faithful.

I was with a Latin woman once having an intimate conversation in her apartment when my cell phone rang. Since the phone was sitting on the coffee table, she picked it up and heard a woman's voice. Would you believe she refused to give me the phone back? She thought I shouldn't talk to another woman when I was with her. I actually had to walk away from the living room once I rescued my phone in order to continue the conversation with the woman in question, who happened to be my daughter. It was embarrassing."

I think this is more an evidence of bad manners than jealousy. You just don't pry into other people's private conversations, whether they happen to be with a man or with a woman. But the fact that we may be less trusting and naïve when it comes to sexual relations might have something to do with knowing what a powerful force sex can be. And it's true that infidelity, while not openly condoned, is many times accepted as a necessary evil in Latin countries, particularly in the case of powerful men.

I was once at a dinner party in Buenos Aires during the days of the Clinton/Monica Lewinsky affair when the ex-president was being interrogated on national television. The program was being broadcast in Argentina and as it happened, the only two people glued to the television set that evening where my husband and myself. The others kept a lively conversation going in the adjoining dining room.

"Who cares if he slept with another woman," finally asked one of the guests, annoyed at the fact that we couldn't stay away from the TV, "the question is, is he a good president?" And everybody else agreed.

As it happened, it was a known fact that their own president at the time, Carlos Menem, was having his own marital problems, and in fact fathered a child out of wedlock with a female member of Parliament. The going joke was: "if his wife wants to be the first lady... she has to wake up very early in the morning..." But Menem is not the only Latin American president to admit to extramarital affairs. Bolivia's Evo Morales and Paraguay's Fernando Lugo also had paternity suits brought upon them during their presidency.

South Carolina's Governor Mark Sanford's affair with an Argentine woman caused a stir back home, but Argentines don't get as worked up about political scandals as Americans do, and in fact tolerate infidelity among their politicians "as long as it's not too ostentatious," according to Sara Moscona, an Argentine psychologist who wrote a book on infidelity. "Argentines are more flexible and forgiving," she said.

We're not saying that you should accept your husband's infidelity. Or that other women will not try to sway him, particularly if he is a highly desirable man. The idea is to avoid the possibility of having him stray by having the man of your dreams value you to the extent that he will not jeopardize losing you... even though he might be tempted. You can't—nor do you want—to keep a man under constant surveillance. But the fact that he is putting your relationship in danger if he gets involved with another woman should be enough of a deterrent, if he truly loves you—and if you keep him fascinated and excited by constantly showing him different aspects of you.

Dave feels that American men cheat less because a great deal of their energy gets spent at work and playing sports. Latin men once they pass their prime are not so much into sports. (That does not include watching soccer, about which they are rabid fans.) "Besides," he tells me, "when I was married, sex became such an uninspiring endeavor that I actually lost my taste for it!" How sad!

The good news is that Dave is now happily dating a very pretty Brazilian who has him running home every night after work with stars in his previously jaded eyes.

Formality is Not Our Strong Suit

One recurring theme in the women I have interviewed is that they don't stand on ceremony. Latins are impulsive people. We organize a party on the spot and everybody comes. Even if we hear about it at the last minute, our feelings don't get hurt. We simply go with the flow. All we really need is music, a few drinks and plenty of food and we're on.

Informality also extends to the way we relate to other people. It doesn't take long for a Latin to bring you into his/hers close circle of friends if they like you and that, of course, will extend to their family members as well. So if you happen to hit if off with a Latin woman, you will automatically be considered "simpatico" to cousins, siblings and even mom and dad, until you prove them wrong.

I remember being invited to a Christmas party in Los Angeles by close friends of my ex-husband. These were good, hard-working Cuban people and since they loved my ex, whom they had practically adopted while he lived in California, when dinner came they went all the way and brought out a whole roasted pig with an apple in the mouth as the *piece-de-resistance*. My two young children, who were brought up in a Jewish home, had never seen a roasted pig before—and much less the whole animal brought to the table—and quickly hid in the bedroom until it was time to go home. Well, these people meant well...

Informality can also get carried away at times. Years ago I attended a wedding in Mexico City. Halfway through the ceremony I noticed that guests were quietly leaving the chapel. I couldn't figure out why until I stepped out once the ceremony was over. Wherever I looked in the beautifully decorated ballroom there were chairs leaning against the tables.

When I asked one of the guests why that was the case, he told me they had been coming out and leaning the chairs in this manner in order to reserve them for themselves and their friends, since there was no arranged seating. Realizing what I was up against, I had to go through the humiliating task of going from table to table asking if there was an empty seat...So much for informality!

Last year I went back for another party in Mexico City and lo and behold, I was handed a place card with the table number neatly inscribed. Thank God we're learning!

18

We Love to Spoil Him

ake a group of Latin women and ask them what in their opinion sets them apart in their approach to men and they will say in unison: "*los consentimos*", "we spoil them." And it's true. We really spoil our men.

Ask any man married to a Latin woman and he will agree. What do we do for them?

We cook for them. Cooking may be a dying art in industrialized countries like the U.S., but Latin women still love cooking for their men. It is a way to express our creativity and our love, particularly by indulging them with their favorite dishes.

We choose their clothes. Many a Latin wife is responsible for her husband's wardrobe. We love to see him well dressed. Shorts and T-shirts are not our favorite attire for the men we love. Linen pants and silk shirts are.

We keep a tidy, beautiful home. Few Latin men will walk into a messy home. We pride in keeping an immaculate environment for our family.

We buy them their favorite cologne. I still remember walking hand in hand with my mother to the House of Guerlain in Havana's Paseo del

Prado (the equivalent of Barcelona's Ramblas) to buy my father a bottle of Guerlain's Blue Ribbon cologne. It was her traditional Valentine's Day gift, which he used to splash every morning on his handkerchief before going to work. He did love the fresh citrusy scent, but it was also my mother's favorite fragrance on *him*.

We have our special terms of endearment to refer to them like "*papi*," "*mi amor*" or "*cariño*," usually whispered into their eager ears. And our men love hearing every one of them. "Whenever Antonio is away on a business trip and I want him to come home all I have to say is: '*Papi*, I miss you so much!'" my friend Norma tells me with a glint in her dark eyes. "It always works."

What else do we do?
We save the best seat in the house for them.
We let them do the honors at the dinner table
We stay by their side at a cocktail party
We laugh at their jokes...even if we're hearing them for the twentieth time
We treat them with respect.

19

Never Split a Bill

As much as we spoil our men, there is one thing that a Latin woman will not do. We will spoil, honor and obey our men, but we won't split a bill in a restaurant. It's part of the culture: man the protector, the provider; woman the soft, nurturing presence that will attract him, succor and respect him.

The Latin culture still sees the man as the provider and no Latin man will bend so low as to allow a woman to pay while he is around. Don't we take care of him at home? Listen to all his troubles with a compassionate ear, no matter what time of day— or night? Don't we cook for him, keep an immaculate home for him and give him the best seat in the house? He, in turn, takes care of us in the material world.

Even in these enlightened times when women work out of the house and earn sometimes as much as a man, we still expect the man to perform according to his role.

Paying for dinner or lunch is part of the price he pays for having the pleasure of your company, for going out and being seen with such a princess, for being the beneficiary of all your charms. The more you think this way, the more you will place yourself in the exalted place you need to be, and if he is the prince that you deserve, he will see it that way also.

As long as things work out as they were designed ages ago, the differences between the sexes will be emphasized and everybody will be happy. If you want to be considerate about his finances because you are not sure of what he can afford, suggest an inexpensive place when you go out to dinner. And if you feel that you must reciprocate, you can buy him a gift or cook him a wonderful meal at your place. That is what is gender appropriate and will bring both of you eternal happiness. Leave other behavior to your liberated friends, who by now have probably gotten used to having dinner alone.

Paying for dinner is part of what a man needs to do to enjoy the pleasure of the company of an enchantress like you. So go ahead and let him enjoy. Don't deprive him of the pleasure of "taking you out." Even the expression indicates what is expected: he is the one that is taking you out, not the other way around—and don't you forget it!

We Are Not Aggressive

We said it before. A Latin woman's approach to her man, even if she is the initiator, is subtle and never direct. She will make sure to catch his attention, but the signs are always non-verbal:

A sideway glance
A toss of hair
A dazzling smile
The way she dresses. Undoubtedly to capture a man's attention—no power suits please.
The way she walks. Remember all that hip swinging?
The way she reaches out to hold a drink. Slow...and deliberate
The way she dances when she's not yet dancing with him
The way she dances when she's dancing with him
The way she smells. Delicious...

A Latin woman will rarely step out of her house without proper "packaging": Hair, nails, makeup perfectly in place. Because "*you never know who you're going to meet at the meat counter.*"

Since our culture abhors aggressive women, placing them in the same category as innocuous men, we can only win a man over by the power of attraction, and we make doubly sure that we *are* attractive to him.

Lucky is the man who ends up ensnared in the embracing web of such a woman, for she will rarely revert to neglect once she has him. I still remember my mother showering and getting all dolled up just before my father came home from work. "Your father is coming" meant clean up and look your best. Therefore from a very tender age I understood the importance of looking good around the opposite sex.

The other side of that command was that once I cleaned up and put on a clean outfit I was not allowed to go out and play any more, I just had to sit pretty....*booooring*! But to this day once I'm dressed to go out I try to stay in an air conditioned room not to get messed up.

Do we care about presentation? You bet!

20

Welcome to "El Grupo"

One of the pillars of my life has always been my many friends. Friends add humor, insight and support. One of the things that have kept me anchored in Miami has been my extensive social circle that not only includes acquaintances, but a significant number of good friends. Whenever there has been an opportunity to move to a different locale, no matter how enticing the proposition, the fact that I will be away from my cherished support system prevails, and I stay.

I find that having a big social circle is the backdrop against which my life unfolds. And if a new man would come into play I found it necessary that he interacted with and became part of that circle, which includes not only my family, but those around me that I have shared experiences with throughout most of my life.

The truth remains that after the first few months of intensity when a couple might want to be alone most of the time to revel in the wonder of discovery, we all need other people. And having a network of good friends with whom we can spend time and bring our beloved into can only enrich the relationship. We call this "*el grupo*", the group.

I have found this to be a positive force, and generally if a man likes me and we are a good fit, he ends up liking my friends. Having a relationship where you have to exclude your friends or even worse, make excuses for your boyfriend generally does not bode well for the future, and having parties to go to and places to visit adds an extra dimension to a relationship, unless you happen to be involved with an introvert, which presents its own set of problems.

Latin people tend to be gregarious and usually a new person gets a hearty welcome into the social circle. *El grupo* usually begins in high school and continues through the rest of our lives, constantly adding new acquaintances here and there to the original core. It becomes sort of a real-life Facebook without a wall that you can always fall back on when life pitches a hard ball—and an instant party list when you have something to celebrate. I recently had a birthday and ended up celebrating the occasion four times: first with one group of women friends, twice with two other groups of friends and once with a significant other who happens to be an American.

"I can't understand this," he told me over drinks, the day of my real birthday, which I spent with him, "I would be lucky if my kids take me out on my birthday, let alone find three different sets of friends to go out with!"

The fun, support and acceptance that this group brings into a union can only count as a positive element, and many an American man has even kept the Latin woman's friends in case of a split off, so treasure your friends even more when there is a new man in your life. See them as anchors of your emotional life who will validate and support you and your new love. And the fact that you have many people who know you and like you will only add to your allure in the eyes of your beloved. After all, nobody wants a girl who nobody likes.

21

Accentuate the positive and other good traits

Yes, I know, you've been married for thirty years and those evenings cuddled up in front of the TV set watching basketball games or reruns of the Discovery channel are getting kind of old. You already know by heart the mating rituals of Rhesus monkeys and why elephants travel in packs. You want to go out on the town for a nice dinner and a movie, or perhaps catch a new Broadway play. But your man cannot be moved away from the couch. He is just so comfy! You're torn between feeling tenderness—after all, he does work hard—and exasperation. This is Friday night, after all! But before you start building up a grudge because he doesn't even send you flowers any more and life is kind of humdrum—not to mention that he loves to argue for any little thing, why don't you stop and remember the way it used to be. Back when, when you first met.

When couples go for therapy the first thing they are asked is to remember what attracted them to each other in the first place. If you can bring back those good feelings that we tend to forget as years go by and we start to take them for granted, things suddenly brighten up. Like the way he used to look at you across the breakfast table when you first got married, or the tone of his voice when he said "good night baby" before dozing off to sleep. Perhaps it was the first time he sent you a dozen long-stemmed bright pink roses with a card saying: "Just because."

In the rush and monotony of everyday life we tend to forget all the good warm feelings that a close relationship with another human being can provide. Never underestimate them. This is really what life is all about. The other stuff: the vacations, the parties, the social part is all icing on the cake and part and parcel of a happy life together but remember, the emphasis should be in the "together". No man is an island, and neither is a woman... we all need each other to feel complete.

Be appreciative

He may be as rich as Crasus or a nine to five Joe, it doesn't matter. The fact that he thinks enough of you to pick out a thoughtful present is all that counts and whether it is a single red rose, a bottle of your favorite perfume or a diamond ring, delight in his offering. It will make him want to bring you more. The fact that he can please you will make him feel ten feet tall. And if you can make it a habit to point out all his good qualities in front of his friends and everyone else you meet, I can guarantee you will have a happy man for the rest of your life. That, by the way, is the secret of many enchanting women who, even though they may not be particularly attractive, seem to have their men eating out of their hand. They just know the way to make a man feel validated.

What is their secret? Saying things like: "Steven is the one holding that company together. I don't know what they would do without him." Or "George is so handy we never need a handyman. He can fix anything!" And "Could you find someone more thoughtful than my Danny? Whenever I work overtime, by the time I come home the table is already set and dinner is on the way. He's one in a million."

Appreciation is like sea foam, it elevates the person who receives it to new heights and the person who gives it acquires a golden patina in the eyes of the beholder. After all, don't you like someone who is always complimenting you? It's a two-way street. You give, you receive, and everyone is happy. But there is something more— by creating mutual feelings of good will, you start cementing a relationship that will stand the test of time. For there is more than looks and personality into play; there is trust and knowing that in times of good or bad you have a stalwart companion by your side to comfort and sustain you. Humans are not meant to be alone. Even in the wild, animals bond together, sometimes, like in the case of a swan, for life. If a swan loses its mate, you will see it swimming alone, the one fellow in the pond without a partner.

We Feel His Pain

Empathy is the ability to "feel his pain," and Latins in general are compassionate, feeling-oriented people. When it comes to the man-woman relationship, it is a rare Latin woman who will not run to her man in time of need. The other day I was talking to a very gifted Peruvian painter who recently started seeing an Argentinean professor quite a bit older than her. She is as taken with his wit and intellect as he is with her artistic sensibility, and they are beginning to establish a very pleasant relationship.

As luck would have it the poor man needed a knee and hip operation shortly after they met and decided to have it done in Philadelphia to be near his daughter. The day before his flight Marcela boarded up her apartment to protect it against the onslaught of an approaching tropical storm and went up to Armando's house to help him pack. "I feel so bad for him. All that pain and the recuperation away from home. I may fly up to see him," she told me, close to tears.

Whether this develops into something serious only time will tell, but I can assure you this much: this man will forever remember what Marcela is doing for him. In times of need we see who our friends are... and our lovers.

Gregg, an American happily married to a Cuban woman for over thirty years, sums it up this way: "Latin women have a heart; they are compassionate, they feel for you." Gregg fell in love with Norma at first sight. "She was sitting in the back seat of a car with a friend of mine one evening in Miami when we were supposed to double date to bring me out of seclusion after a difficult divorce. I took one look at Norma and asked my friend to move to the front. I wanted to sit next to *her*."

Gregg tells me that he loves talking to Norma. "She has intelligence and wit, but most importantly, whatever she has to say she says in a very sweet manner. She is also very giving of her time and of herself. What can I say? I had no choice but to fall in love with her."

Kindness, the quality of your contribution, has as much to do with the success of your relationship as anything else that goes into it, or into your life, for that matter. There is an old Chinese proverb: "a little bit of fragrance always clings to the hand that gives you roses." When you give, some of that goodness sticks with you to enhance and uplift your life, so put yourself on the line time and again and see your well being bloom in more ways than one.

At the risk of sounding like a Pollyanna, giving is its own reward, simply because the act carries a built-in satisfaction that is intuitive and life-affirming, if for no other reason than the fact that we're all in this together. Today I may give to you, tomorrow may be my turn to receive. By giving to others you simply open up the channels of cooperation that keep the cobwebs of selfishness away.

But giving of yourself carries another bonus. Goodness is the fertilizer that, once poured into a relationship, enriches the soil in unforeseen ways to make it bloom with all kinds of wonderful feelings that will feed the two of you for years to come. So go ahead and give, the rewards will have no choice but to multiply.

22

Do you Really like Men?

This may sound like a silly question, but it's not. Some women start from a place of hate in relating to men. They may have come from a dysfunctional home. In these days, who hasn't? Or may have had a traumatic experience in a relationship that has scarred them for life.

Those women will subconsciously sabotage any attempt to carry on a healthy relationship with a man. To them I say run, don't walk to the nearest counselor and get yourself on track, for a woman like this has the word "hate" branded on her forehead. A man can see it a mile away-and will run in the opposite direction.

My friend Estela went into a deep depression after a nasty divorce from a philandering husband left her reeling with low self-esteem. Finally at the urging of her friends who couldn't listen to another "that bastard" story, she posted her profile on an Internet site and hoped for the best. But after three months of lukewarm dates that led nowhere she got some good counseling, lost thirty pounds and posted a new picture.

She got forty responses in two weeks and is now happily interviewing prospective boyfriends. When I asked what prompted her new attitude her answer was: "The moment I started focusing on myself instead of my hate for Ricardo everything changed. I realized that I also had a right to find love... and I could only do that by making the best of what I had."

And then Estela did something I had never seen her do. With a sly smile and a twinkle in her eye she confessed that the man she had met the night before had invited her to sail around the world in his new sailboat. Of course, she did not accept yet... she's going bowling with someone new tomorrow! In other words, she's enjoying her time with men... and slowly learning to like them again.

A woman who loves men-and I don't mean this in a promiscuous way, but rather in a wholesome, playful manner-radiates with excitement every time she runs into an attractive member of the opposite sex. She's relaxed and accepting, and has a refreshing lightness about her. For a woman like this the man-woman thing is like a game she has learned to play to perfection. She's infused with a sense of humor that makes every encounter fun. An afternoon looking at old photographs, a walk on the beach, even a trip to the supermarket become fun with a woman like this. A man gets the feeling that there is no ulterior motive when she is with him. And it's true, for she really enjoys his company.

She's a playful companion. And if there is something men of all ages like to do is play. Football, baseball, basketball, to name just a few are men's passions. Not to mention tennis, golf, backgammon...Should I go on?

Keep things light and easy and you will never want for male company. Find the humorous edge to every situation and you will laugh your way together to a beautiful friendship and more... When you become some-one he can play with, he will look forward to every encounter. He may even buy a ticket!...To Paris, perhaps?

Life is not Fair

We said before that men fall in love with what they see, women with what they hear. My thirty-year old son has just come home from a date.

(He's living temporarily with me) and when I ask him how the date went he blurts out: "Terrible!"

"Terrible?" I repeat, alarmed. "What was wrong with the girl?" and my mind starts racing as I imagine all sorts of uncomfortable situations that my pride and joy might have had to endure during the course of the evening.

Finally he looks at me as if the sky were falling as he takes out a bottle of soda from the refrigerator and exclaims:

"She was fat!"

"Fat?" I repeat like an idiot, stunned by his answer, but suddenly relieved. She didn't get drunk, hit him with an enormous dinner bill or punctured his tires. She was just fat. And then it hits me. The unfairness of it all.

Did he say anything about her personality?

Or whether or not they had things in common?

Or whether he enjoyed the conversation?

No. All he said was that she was fat.

That was enough. Had she been slimmer, prettier or taller things might have progressed to another level, but the sad reality is that men go for looks first.

That is why I dedicated several chapters of this book to your grooming. And why you should always strive to look the very best you can, even if you're just going to the corner drugstore to buy a pain killer. You never know what kind of prince might be hiding behind that shallow exterior.

A woman, on the other hand, will go over every word her new man uttered during the date, looking for clues to his feelings and trying to analyze any hidden meanings that may lead to a further commitment on his part. Did he hint at a vacation together next Christmas? Why else would he have commented on the time share his family owns in Telluride?

He did mention his sister was going to be in town next week. Does that mean he wants you to meet her? She may lull herself to sleep imagining going down the slopes with him on a sunny Colorado afternoon, his beaming sister waiting at the bottom of the mountain with a cup of hot chocolate in her hand. Such is our need for bonding and the power of the female imagination.

And if she's talking with him on the phone, his voice will carry her to new heights of ecstasy, if it's the right voice. Men who know how to use this power can successfully woo any woman they want. No wonder volumes of poetry have been written for star-crossed lovers and an eloquent man is so highly prized, no matter what he looks like.

The first time I talked on the telephone with my second husband I envisioned him as being six foot tall, dark and handsome; such was the power of his well modulated voice, which he used to its full advantage. Imagine my disillusionment when he turned out to be five foot five and not particularly attractive. But he kept talking to me and I fell for him, although I must say that the best part of the relationship was the long-distance courting with all those all-night romantic conversations when he whispered sweet nothings in my ear all the way from Los Angeles.

Don't Listen to What He Says; Pay Attention to What He Does

Even the smartest woman falls pray every once in a while to a womanizer.

These are men who set out to prove one point: that they can seduce women.

Unfortunately these men make a career out of understanding the woman's psyche and are tuned into what makes us tick with the same sensitivity of a virtuoso playing a Stradivarius.

They do their homework well, and, knowing that a woman falls in love with what she hears, will be happy to oblige and tell you exactly what you want to hear. But if you listen carefully, you will notice that he always talks in the future tense. "You are only going to have one problem with me: I have two left feet" or: "When we visit Oregon you are going to love the coastline" as if he has your future mapped out for the rest of your lives.

You, hopeful creature that you are, are ready to start packing, but there is only one element missing in all this conversation: a definite date. For the trip, for the dance... everything remains—like an inveterate womanizer once told me, referring to an ex-girlfriend—"in promise land." In some nebulous never never land that, unfortunately, is as the name implies, never going to happen.

But as long as you keep hearing these wonderful tidbits of information, you are going to keep believing simply because you want to believe. These wonderful promises are the fuel that keeps the womanizer's cart going, with you in it, in that hazy, if comfortable—at least for him—"promise land." However, as time goes on, you are going to start feeling the bumps on the road, for this is a land that, I guarantee you, you'll never set foot on.

Therefore, promise me that from now on you will listen to what he says, but follow up by paying very close attention to what he does. If one does not match the other, do yourself a favor and leave. If nothing else, your quick action will be enough of a shock to his system that he may start delivering; but if I were you, I would look for greener pastures.

This type of man does not wear well and, like an ill-fitting beautiful pair of shoes will only look good on the outside, but will end up hurting you inside. Life is too short to endure any kind of unnecessary pain.

Be Independent

Yes, I know, I have told you to be feminine and caring, and now I'm telling you to be independent. Well, one does not contradict the other.

An independent woman will have a full life with or without a man. By that I mean that you are not sitting waiting and praying that the phone will ring and it will be him. You have a life that includes a job, hopefully one that you enjoy and are good at. That in itself will nurture and fulfill you; a family that will provide you with companionship, fill your holidays and support you when the going gets rough, and good friends that will be there to listen, share good and bad times and just plain have fun.

An independent woman is a relatively new phenomenon in our society. Until just a few decades ago this was the realm of a few fortunate women who either had the vision to pursue a career or had independent means. Luckily today working—for a woman— has become the norm rather than the exception.

Contrary to what you might think, Latin women are well aware of this fact and many successful women in America happen to be Latin. Such is the case of Cristina, the Latin equivalent of Oprah who has a daily TV show and also runs her own magazine, Ileana Ros- Lehtinen, the first Hispanic woman ever elected to the U.S. Congress, and Sonia Sotomayor, the first Hispanic Supreme Court justice, as well as countless real estate professionals, lawyers and physicians who have measured up to the opportunities that America offers. And in countries like Chile, Uruguay and Argentina, which have had a higher number of European immigrants from places like Italy and Germany besides Spain, there is a very high percentage of professional women.

During my years as a staff writer for Spanish Goodhousekeeping my editor was Pilar Larrain, a Chilean journalist with an impressive career in her native Santiago.

In my case, my mother drummed up into me from a very tender age the importance of having a career to retain my independence, no matter what life happened to bring, which over the years has proven to be invaluable advice.

Why is it then that I dedicate a whole chapter to this subject? Because, ironically, even though many of us have careers and pay our own bills, we still hold on to the wonderful illusion that a knight in shining armor is going to whisk us away from all this drudgery and ensconce us in his castle. Well, he might just do that, but believe me when I tell you, he will be much more inclined to do so if he believes that you don't need him.

Here we go again with the challenge bit. A woman who is secure in her own world and doesn't need to be rescued will be much harder to get than one who is waiting by the curbside. And men, competitive creatures that they are, are hardwired to look for the more difficult tasks, which is what they appreciate and work hard to get.

If you are not available to take his phone call because you are busy with a client, he will learn to schedule his calls according to your convenience. If you have a deadline and cannot see him on Friday night, he will respect the fact that your time is as valuable as his. The more evidence you give him that you have a full, meaningful life without him, the more he will value you for what you are without him, and the more he will prize winning you over. Remember the competitive nature of men: the more enticing the goal, the more worthy the pursuit. Don't play hard to get—remember we don't play games—but *be* hard to get, simply because you're worth it.

So be well grounded, busy and successful and go through life like the amazing creature that you are. Let your days be filled with purpose and, if that knight comes by, let him go a few rounds on his horse before he can catch you; he will appreciate his true princess for the rest of his very lucky life.

Don't Waste your Time with Someone Who Doesn't Appreciate What You Do

When a man is in love with you—and this is the only kind you should consider as a mate—he will pay attention to what is important to you; he will want to know what makes you tick, and everything that emanates from you will be precious. If you confess that your mother favored your little brother over you, he will bring it out months later in conversation; if you like chocolate-covered strawberries, he will make sure to bring home some just to delight you.

In short, you—and everything related to you—will be relevant to him. This is a good way to test whether the man you're involved with has what it takes to make you happy. Many women, intent on finding a man—any man—forget that in a relationship happiness has to flow in both directions: he has to make *you* happy too.

Estela was a gifted writer involved with an international businessman. At the beginning of their whirlwind courtship —they met at a consular dinner and he didn't stop calling her since—she used to leave copies of her newspaper column in his home office, on top of his desk, for him to read. These were columns in which she used to pour her heart out and express some very insightful tidbits of her life's philosophy, and her intention was for him to get to know her better through her writing and find out what really moved her.

Interestingly enough, whenever she visited his apartment, she used to make a quick dash to his office to see if he had read the column, but the papers were always neatly arranged in the same spot. It was clear he had not even bothered to pick them up and he never made any reference to her writing either. Weeks went by and she kept her curiosity at bay, until she couldn't hold back her frustration any longer and finally confronted him.

"Have you read the columns I left on your desk last month?' she asked one evening as they were watching the news, rather annoyed at his obvious dismissal of her life's work. "You know," he answered taking her hand in his, "I'm waiting for you to read them to me."

While writing was what defined her, this man wouldn't even make the effort of reading what came out of her innermost musings, the seat of her soul. Estela went on to marry the man, for she was deeply in love with him, and enjoyed seven years of constant travels and a very active social life, but in the end his lack of sensitivity grated on her writer's soul and she left him.

The moral of the story: if what you do is of no interest to him, he is either an outdated chauvinist who thinks women's work is unimportant (there are still some of those around) or an insensitive clod. Either way, you shouldn't waist your precious time on him. Look for someone who will appreciate you for what you are and who will take pride in what you do. You will be a lot happier with that kind of man, even if you just sit home and watch television with him—it may just be what you really want to do.

How to Know when a Man is Falling in Love with You

When he lovingly touches your hair and your hands; when he kisses your eyes, your forehead, the tip of your nose. When he looks at your face with unbridled longing. These are all displays of tenderness, which is a step up from pure lust. When a man concentrates on your face, your hair, your eyes, he is focusing on the ethereal part of you, your true essence, and that is what he will fall in love with. If he grabs your arms, your legs or any other body part you should stop him immediately; these are misdirected displays of affection and are only permissible within the context of an ongoing mature love relationship, definitely not during courtship. Your face, your voice, the things you say are what are going to elicit his feelings of love, what he will slowly start to become attached to—with emphasis on the word slowly. Your body, on the other hand, will attract his lust--fast.

Even though both are needed for lasting love to bloom, during the time of courtship and until you have a better idea where the relationship is going, you should maximize what you say and minimize what you do (remember Scheherazade.) For it is through the exchange of feelings and ideas that you are going to connect as two human beings capable of deeply caring for one another. It is this foundation what will ensure the future of your relationship with the man you love.

Man's attention span is very short when it comes to satisfying his sexual urges. If you succumb to his advances before cementing a good relationship, once he gets to know all there is to know about you, he will set sail to conquer new territories. You want to be that island where he sets down his anchor, not just another entry in his log.

Accept Graciously That One of You Has to Travel Shortly After You Meet.

Suppose you meet in the summer, really hit if off and lo and behold, you or he had previously made travel plans. Should you curse all travel agents and settle in for a miserable time while you are away from your new love? *Au contraire!* This could actually work in your favor. You see, if you really made an impression on him, this forced time away from you will end up increasing his longing. Suddenly you will become his fair maiden, and like Romeo and Juliet, separated by external forces, he will wish nothing more than to see you soon after his return.

A good friend just ran into that situation. She had started seeing a very eligible widower who was still grieving the passing of his beloved wife. They were getting along quite well; they both had artistic natures and were enjoying theater and dancing outings, when he suddenly announced that he had planned a cruise to Europe with his children six months before and was leaving in two weeks. After the initial shock (she really had started to like him a lot) Gisela, instead of sulking, encouraged him to go, suggested places to visit and even bought him a going-away gift. We don't know where all this will end, but a week into the cruise she received this email from him: "This cruise has many misses: miss your face, miss your voice, miss your dancing..." Mmm the romance is humming along.

23

Stop Competing with Your Man

In this competitive world we live in we tend to view everyone as an adversary, and this sometimes extends to the men in our lives. Yes, even without being aware of it you may be trying to out smart, out talk and out do the man you promised to love, honor and obey. If you are a career woman it may be difficult, if not impossible, to separate the way you act with colleagues in the business world with the way you interact with the man who shares your life.

Well, if you want a happy relationship that will stand the test of time, do yourself a favor and step out of the competitive treadmill for a minute. Now stop and appreciate him for what he is: a member of the opposite sex who will fill in the empty spaces that all your other blessings: friends, career and family, no matter how fulfilling, cannot.

A good relationship is like a key fitting into a keyhole. Each notch is perfectly cut to fit into the specific groove that will accommodate it. Once the fit is in place, you will together be able to open the door to the precious intimacy and exalted times that only the love between a man and a woman can bring.

Am I asking you to stop being a modern woman? By no means. All I'm asking is not to forget that beyond career, success and ambition you are first and foremost a woman, with needs that only a man can fulfill.

In the years when I used to publish a city magazine I met an extremely successful tax attorney. "You know what I like most about you?" he told me one night over drinks at a trendy Coconut Grove club, "the fact that even though you are in a very competitive business, you have managed to maintain your femininity." And yes, I had to deal with deadlines, distribution, salespeople and printing headaches, but when evening came I put on my high heels and became a total woman. I wouldn't trade my experience as such with any other kind of success, no matter what the monetary rewards would have been. What has kept me grounded, happy and soulfully alive all these years was always my role as a woman. And even today, when I no longer have a business, I revel in the fact that I can still keep the man in my life happily by my side—and many others who are not, still aware of my existence.

Did you ever dread the fact that one day you might become invisible? I'm not referring to science fiction, but to the day when construction workers will stop whistling as you walk by, the mailman will hand out your mail without flirting a bit with you first, and the older gentleman at the post office will no longer look at you appreciatively and let you go first. Just because.

When I was younger I used to place that day of reckoning well into my fifties, and now that I passed that deadline by a good ten years, I keep pushing it forward... and doing everything I can to keep it in the distant future. The good news is that today women can look and feel young well into what used to be considered a ripe old age. What we know now about good nutrition, exercise and cosmetic procedures is just part of a modern woman's bag of tricks.

The other element, which is just as important, and one that a Latin woman never forgets, is the right attitude; one that announces to the world that we are having a grand old time just by being on the planet... and can't wait to find out what each new day will bring. Part of it of course is the fact that whenever we leave the house we do it properly packaged:

you know: hair in place, nails, perfume, etc. and carry this feeling of preparedness wherever we go.

For a woman, looking good is nine tenth of the battle, and knowing that you are at your best will even prompt a bit of flirting on your part assured that it will be well received. And so you can go on having fun as a woman even if you are "a woman of a certain age," which is how the French refer to women after 50, when it is difficult to determine the exact age of a well-preserved female.

I find that, in addition, being engaged with life on a one-to-one basis, not only through my children, is what does it for me. Having a project in the making, whether it is writing a book, taking a new course at the university, attending a yoga class or volunteering at the local hospital will keep you young and alert for many years to come... and your children—and grandchildren—proud of having a mother and grandmother like you!

24

Dating the Widower

Many women think that a widower is a much better candidate for a relationship than a single or divorced man. After all, he has had a steady marriage that unfortunately ended due to the death of his wife. If he had a good marriage he probably has what it takes to form another quality relationship. Not so fast.

There is another element that has to be taken into consideration and that at times may make him more difficult to date than a commitment-phobic serial dater. I'm referring to his ability to get over the mourning for his late wife.

A recent widower (anywhere between six months and two years) tends to jump into a relationship with a woman for the simple fact that he misses the companionship he had in his marriage. In effect what he's doing is simply plugging you into the slot that his wife used to occupy in his life.

He will call you three to four times a day and want to spend every waking hour in your company. For the woman this feels like what she had always wanted: a man who is not scarred by divorce or flawed relationships and who is ready to make her the center of his life. He may even utter those sacred words: "I love you" way before he is truly ready to honor them. After a night when you think you are starring in a romantic movie, when he looks into your eyes and tells you: "I adore you", be ready for the disclaimer that follows: "How could I tell you I love you after 20, 30 (you fill in the blanks) years of loving my wife...?"

What is at work here is guilt. If the marriage was good and long lasting this man is caught up in a seesaw of emotions that he may not very well be able to control. He is battling his attraction to you while he is still mourning the death of a beloved partner. In the meantime you are living two realities. One day he's madly in love with you and the next day he pulls away horrified by feelings he is trying to suppress.

You, particularly if you have a background of being a giving and understanding partner, will be tempted to console him and try to make him see that he has to move on with his life, with you acting as the balm that will soothe his wound. But beware, by staying in the relationship at this point you will be pulled by a roller coaster of emotions and in essence will be living in two different realities: One day he is madly in love with you and the next day his guilt will prompt him to pull away. In time, you may even begin to feel like "the other woman," and you would not be mistaken. This man is still emotionally married to his late wife.

You are really trying to hold on to a mirage, for his love seems real to you but is nothing more than an illusion for him. Living in two realities is not too different to what happens to a schizophrenic. In psychological parlance it is called schizophrenogenic behavior and in fact has the capacity to drive you crazy.

If you find yourself involved with a widower, first find out if he is through grieving. If he's not, the best thing you can do for him and yourself is refer him to a qualified psychotherapist. If you are important enough for him, he should have no reservations accepting the guidance of a professional and give your relationship a fair chance.

25

Dating the Serial Dater

There are men who fall in love at the drop of a hat, but who you will be well advised to avoid—except in certain circumstances. We'll get to that in a minute. Yes, they will fall in love with you, but also with your best friend, your younger sister, the baby sitter and the girl at the supermarket checkout counter. Some of these men make a career out of loving women and they sincerely believe they are in the throes of a grand romance each and every single time. Having said that, there are instances in which even the most roguish, died-in-the-wool womanizer will cave in and start to deeply care for a woman. Such as:

When he meets a woman much younger than himself (anywhere between fifteen and thirty years younger). In this case the difference in ages is such that he starts to develop protective feelings towards her, and if the woman is also mature for her years, things will gel.

Or when he meets a woman who challenges him intellectually besides attracting him physically. I must clarify that physical attraction is a very subjective matter. You may meet the woman this type of man finally fell for and wonder what in the world he saw in her, but trust me on this one, the attraction is definitely there. Perhaps she's rather plump, but he may like this type of body, or has hair like a Medusa that he may find sexy... men are such quirky creatures when it comes to sexual attraction!

Having said that, a woman who can challenge a man intellectually will keep him on his toes and bring out his wit and his competitive nature. But I said before that you shouldn't compete with your man, didn't I? Yes, but there is an area in which competition will be welcome. I'm referring to your capacity to elicit good-natured, albeit perhaps a bit naughty old-fashioned banter. Think of it as a kind of intellectual duel, during which each of you can exhibit your wit and humor. A woman who can make a man think fast, who can keep him wondering what she will come up with next will become in his eyes a fascinating creature, one he will set aside from the rest—and look forward to seeing time and again.

The other, and perhaps more genuine reason for this type of man to let down his guard is when he meets a woman who is so real and giving that she will unearth the tender, deep caring feelings we all harbor deep inside. Such is the case of a very successful trial attorney who, after ten years of happily dating without commitment finally met a recent Latin divorcee ten years his junior, who blew him away with her innate sweetness and giving nature. Such was the attraction, that four days after he met her he had to fly back to his hometown to try a difficult case and flew back to Miami the evening after the trial...to find a home-cooked delicious meal waiting for him.

"Nobody has ever done that for me," he told her with tears in his eyes. "Nobody?" his new love answered, "what about your last relationship? You lived in the same town and dated for over a year!"

"Yes, but we only saw each other on weekends and ended up always going out to restaurants," was his answer.

Imagine. Of all the women this hard-working man had dated, no one had cooked a meal for him in years!

The good news is that he was so touched by that gesture that he invited his new love to a black-tie affair that was to take place the following month in his home town, is already talking of a ski trip for them with her kids and her kids' friends...and even offered to give her private ski lessons, since she doesn't ski.

As luck would have it, it turned out that his birthday was the following week, and after racking her brain for the right gift to give to this man, our girl came up with the idea of having a friend take a picture of the two of them, frame it in a beautiful frame and send it to his office, together with a gift certificate from a local gourmet shop to stock enough items for a beachside picnic. As of this writing we don't know yet where this relationship will end, but one thing is sure—it's headed in the right direction.

Men, particularly very successful men, are not used to being at the receiving end of a relationship, and when a woman shows her caring for them in tangible ways, they allow themselves, perhaps for the first time in years, to show their vulnerability, a crucial ingredient for love feelings to begin to flow.

26

Give Only the Right Way and Learn How to Receive

When you first find yourself in a relationship with a man you love, you may be tempted to give him presents. It just feels so good to give to the one you love! I have told you before that Latin women spoil their men. It's true. But you must learn the right way to give and the right way to spoil. Doing so will make a big difference in the way he will treat you now and in the future.

And what is the right way to give? Only after he has given to you in spades, particularly if you are giving things that cost money. Why? you might say, in these times when women and men often earn as much? Because of the hunter instinct and the fact that he will assign a value to you, and you want that value to be high. I was recently talking to a widower, new to the dating game, who confessed that he wanted to date a woman that his friends would approve of. "Do you think I'm being shallow?" he asked, obviously embarrassed. "No," I replied, "you're being human!"

Men are competitive by nature and they work hard to earn a trophy at the end of the tennis game or a promotion at the end of the deal. If you are in his life, you are that sign of success, that achievement that will herald to the world that he has won you over. You have become for him a valuable commodity.

Alright, it is wonderful to feel appreciated, but you also have all these warm and fuzzy feelings that you want to express. How do you do it?

You give from the heart. As in tenderly rubbing his back at the end of a working day, by listening with compassion about his heartless ex-wife who ran away with his best friend, or by cooking him a great meal. You don't buy tickets to a concert or take him on a cruise for his birthday, at least not until he has taken you to a dozen concerts and more trips than you can count with the fingers of both hands. That doesn't mean that you won't buy him a gift for his birthday—You should spend as much as your budget allows, but even more importantly, pick something meaningful to him or, as in the case of the young divorcee and her attorney boyfriend, something that will bring the two of you closer together, like a picnic basket or anything related to food, in which case you should be extremely generous. Remember, women have always been the purveyors of food and love—and those two things are closely tied together, particularly in the minds of men.

But in general you want to establish a pattern, and that pattern is: he buys you things because you're worth it and the more he buys you things, the more you are worth in his eyes. Plain and simple.

Human beings tend to assign little value to things that are given away, regardless of their intrinsic worth, and if you start buying him presents in addition to what you bring into his life by just being you, you are assigning little value to who you are.

I once had a Persian cat with beautiful blue-gray fur and green eyes. As luck would have it, one day she fooled around with an alley cat and had a litter of half-Persian kittens. They were cute as can be, but I didn't feel like taking care of six cats so I put an ad in the paper to give them away. A week went by without a single inquiry. I called the paper's advertising department to complain and the clerk advised me to change my ad. The following week I had a line outside my door. The new ad read: "half-Persian kittens, twenty dollars each."

The moral of the story is if you give, give, give people will take you for granted— and so will the man in your life. You give, within limits, and only after you get. By the mere fact of being you, you are already giving him a neat little package. Your nurturing, loving sweetness. The beautiful home you keep for him, the children you bear for him, the social environment you carve for both of you. These are all things that a real man will appreciate in the woman in his life, and for which he will be eternally grateful— and inclined to show his appreciation in the form of presents, either big or small.

There are women, however, who never learned how to receive because that is their nature or because that is how they were socialized. Perhaps they grew up in a home where the mother did all the giving and the father the receiving and perhaps the mother was never properly appreciated.

In a good relationship learning how to receive is as important as learning how to give. If your man sends you flowers on Valentine's Day be effusive, but don't act as if you just witnessed the second coming. After all, that is what is appropriate and you are worth it. If you over-react he will think that he gave too much and next time your bouquet will be smaller. Receive with dignity and appreciation and he will know that he struck the right note... and next time he will do as much or better.

I don't want to sound calculating, but this is just human nature. You want to strike a balance, and that balance is: he gives to you out of appreciation for having found a real gem, and you give back. The emphasis should be in the "back". Don't ever initiate the giving, unless you just met and his birthday happens to be before yours, in which case you may buy him an appropriate gift, like his favorite cologne, or, depending on how close you feel at this point, a picture of both on you in a keepsake frame or some other personal item.

But remember, this is just a gesture. If you take him away on a cruise instead, he may think he is too good for you and may end up jumping ship— or carrying on a relationship where you are the grape peeler and he the Sultan—and both are places where you don't want to find yourself. Learn how to receive because you're worth it and he'll have no choice but to install you in the throne he had kept hidden all his life for a woman like you.

27

How to Find Love While Surfing the Net

Once a woman, or a man for that matter, finishes school, if steady work in a company is not part of life, it becomes very difficult to find love. It takes the daily interaction of either school or the work place to nurture a relationship between a man and a woman. On the other hand, career people hardly have enough time to look for a mate, which is in itself a full-time job. Years ago we had matchmakers. Today we have the Internet.

In sites like *match.com*, *eharmony* and *jdate*, people find each other through the magic of instant communication. However, like everything else, some do better than others and there is a science to this game.

First of all, you need to post an excellent picture, preferably one taken by a professional and at least two more, showing you full figure. I don't need to tell you that men are extremely visual and even though you can't judge a book by its cover, without a good picture you don't stand a chance in the competitive world of Internet dating.

Next you need to compose a profile. This is where your personality comes through; your likes and dislikes, what is important for you and the particular quirks that make you an individual. Don't be afraid to blow your own horn, this is not the time nor the place to be modest. Let people know your hidden talents, whether you are a gourmet cook, just ran a marathon or are considered a legal eagle, write it all down and then wait. If you've taken the right steps the emails will come, if for no other reason than the fact that you are a new face.

And what if no one contacts you, or the ones that do are of no interest to you? Then you take the initiative. Here is a place where you don't need to stand on ceremony. You surf the site until you find a man that catches your eye and fulfills your requirements—and then you email *him*. He won't think any less of you. Any man who has ever posted a profile on the Internet will tell you that he receives hundreds of emails. Yes, here like everywhere else in life women outnumber men, therefore it is of vital importance that you derive the ability to stand out from the crowd.

How do you do that? By learning how to write to a man on the net. The surer way to approach a man you like is by zeroing in on something that catches your eye in his profile and asking him a question about it. If he is a wine aficionado, start out by asking which is his favorite red. If he is a doctor, ask him what is his specialty. If he lives in a part of the country you have never visited, ask him what it's like living there.

The rationale is very simple: a question generates the need for an answer and that is exactly what you want. It is the interchange of thoughts and ideas that creates a relationship, and also the fact that you are showing an interest in what is important to him will make him feel appreciated. Here is also the place to deliver witticisms. The fact that you have a quick mind will give you extra points. It shows confidence and promises that you will never be boring—A sure killer of many a relationship.

Should you answer an instant message? That depends on what the picture shows. Generally men will send you an instant message because when you are online your picture flashes on the site and you become more visible, so take advantage of this feature and go on line as much as possible.

When you get an instant message you need to answer on the spot, but try to get some insight about the man in question by reading his profile first, although granted, there are times when there is not enough time to do this. In that case start chatting until you get a clearer idea of who he is. Once you have both established a common ground the man will usually request your phone number —unless he's a killer typist, which most men are not, he will want to proceed to a telephone conversation. At this point, depending on how you feel about the person, you may request his phone number for you to call him if you don't want him to know how to reach you yet, or else if you feel comfortable enough, give him yours. Although frankly, since today most people have caller ID, it doesn't make much difference, except for the fact that if you get his number, you are in control of when the phone call will be made.

Anyway, regardless of who calls whom, once you get him on the phone you have to be attentive to many things. The first one, of course is his voice. Is it well modulated? Some men will be nervous the first time they talk to a woman. That's alright. These probably will be the better ones. The perennial bachelors have had plenty of experience romancing ladies and will sound calm and confident. Remember, practice makes perfect. You want to stay away from them. Others will sound nervous because, regardless of their background or experience with women, find you so attractive and exciting that they lose some control. Still others will be in charge and grounded no matter what. That is also good.

The time on the phone is crucial. This is where you have to know how to conduct a mini-interview without sounding like that is what you're doing. Instead of asking "what do you do for a living?" which places the emphasis on how much money he makes, ask him what is his occupation, which places the emphasis on what he does. The difference is subtle, but important. Men are very sensitive about this subject and you will have to tread very lightly around the issue of money. You also want to know how long he has been single. If it's too soon after he's divorced or widowed he may not be ready for a serious relationship, if that is what you want. If he has been single for too long he may never submit to the bonds of matrimony. Ideally you're looking for a man who has had enough time to get his bearings, usually two to five years into bachelorhood. Depending on how the conversation goes you will go on to a face to face meeting or just dismiss him with a polite "we'll talk again."

Is it alright to date more than one man? The answer is yes, as long as you keep away from intimacy. You don't want to get all mixed up; neither do I believe that you will want to, since once sex gets in the way, women end up wanting to be with a man exclusively. That's the way we are genetically programmed. So until you are sure he is the one, keep it light.

Does Internet dating work? I have gone to several weddings where the couple met this way. Although I must admit we're talking about young professionals in their 30's and early 40's. The older you get, the more difficult it becomes, mostly because of that man/woman ratio. But think of it as entertainment. Exchanging emails and chatting on the phone beats watching *Wheel of Fortune*. You will certainly go out on a few dates, sometimes you end up striking a friendship and, who knows, you might even end up meeting your soul mate.

Take the Bumps with a Smile

Is life going to be peachy once you find the love of your life? It may well be if you are very very lucky, but unfortunately life is not made only of romance and candlelit dinners. Bad things happen: children get sick or misbehave, jobs get lost or businesses go bad, your own or your parents' health demands attention. There are a whole lot of things that can cram your existence with pain and sorrow, but having someone by your side to comfort you and listen to your pain, and offer solace and advice is a tremendous advantage in this sometimes cold, difficult world.

The fact that we go on and greet every day with joy and hope is a miracle that keeps human beings going no matter what life brings. A good dose of optimism can work wonders to turn every day into the true gift God intended it to be. Irritants will be there along the way; they seem to be a part of life. But remembering the good that is present in everybody's life, even in moments of darkest despair, seems to be just the right formula to turn on the light and bring in the music. One good idea in difficult times is to keep a Journal of Gratitude. In it I write every day the things that I can be thankful for. Such as:

The sunny apartment where I live, with the red bougainvillea that I planted years ago steadily winding through the gates of my terrace displaying a sun-kissed riot of color whenever I look out.

My beautiful daughter, who is more a friend and trusted confidant than a daughter. Even as a five-year old she was the responsible one: "Mommy, did you lock the door? Do you have your keys with you?" I guess she realized even then the absent-minded dreamer she was handed as a mother.

The comfortable bed I sleep in, when so many people are homeless in this world.

My trusted friends who are always there for me.

The photo albums I keep full of memories of wonderful times and great trips. Whenever I begin to feel a bit down, I take one out and remind myself of what a great run I've had.

My personal achievements which through the years have brought fulfilling recognition from my peers.

My 50-year high school reunion where everyone still knew me without having to look at the picture in the year book in order to match the face with the name.

As I'm about to put the finishing touches on this book and end what feels like a daily conversation with you, my reader, that I'm going to truly miss, I try to focus on all those blessings, and hope my humble words of wisdom distilled over many years of living will help you find true love, happiness and just plain fun. Life is meant to be shared with another wonderful human being.

Latin women know this and appreciate all the beautiful things that a man can bring into our lives, that's why we treasure, spoil and love to pieces the ones who come to share ours. Men and women, as difficult as it sometimes may seem to be, are meant to be together. The good news is that when the right one shows up, things just flow. There are no books, including this one that can teach you how to manufacture love and create a relationship where there is no solid base for one.

I was recently attending a wedding when a young friend pulled me aside.

"I need to ask you a question," she said, her pretty face serious with concern. The ballroom where the reception was being held was extremely noisy and we went outside into the hallway so that we could talk.

She had started seeing a man who professed his interest in her and wanted to bring their relationship to the next level. The problem? She wasn't sure she wanted to do so. "There is something missing," she told me and I could see it in her eyes. "Do you think that with time I could come to love him?"

"Well. The answer is: it depends what kind of love you're after," I said. The wedding we were attending was that of a bachelor who had finally found the love of his life at forty six, and you could feel the energy in that room, full of friends of the bride and groom who didn't stop dancing and crowding around the happy couple.

"Look Cynthia," I asked her taking a peek at the ballroom, "don't you want to feel the same way when you get married?"

"Yes," she said, misty eyed, "I really do. I want my wedding day to be the happiest day of my life." Then, at the risk of sounding like a fairy Godmother I told her that she was too young to compromise and to wait until the real thing came around.

"Your prince will come," I said. "When that happens you won't need me to make your decision, you'll just *know*."

Waiting for love to materialize out of an anemic relationship has never happened to me, it won't happen to Cynthia and I don't think will happen to you. When love finds you, those same feelings you may be confused about now will flow without you even having to think about them. Love is easy. The difficult part is finding it. May yours come quickly to brighten your life and fill up all the empty spaces. I wish you love.

Epilogue

A Word to Men: What do Women Want?

For centuries men have pondered this question when the answer is really so simple. *Women want to feel protected.* I know, what about these last thirty years? The problem, fellows, is that in the past you have gotten carried away in what you call "protection." We don't need to be protected against using our brain, otherwise God would not have given us one. But even if a woman can fly to the moon, she still prefers to fall asleep with a pair of strong arms wrapped around her soft skin. Men who know this have always been attractive to women.

What else do women want? They want to feel like women. And no woman can feel like a real woman unless there is a man around her that makes her feel like one. Some men have a way of looking at a woman and making her feel entirely female. They have a very subtle way of relating, a glint in their eye that makes a woman feel all warm and tingly. These are the most attractive men of all. They don't necessarily have to be physically attractive, they don't even have to act on it, but the strength of their manliness oozes out through every pore.

The late Humphrey Bogart had that quality and so does George Clooney and Bill Clinton... and it shows!

Women want to Feel Special

Men spend thousand of dollars buying presents for their women and then they complain that they're not appreciated. But it's not how much you spend, fellows, it's how you give that's important.

My first husband used to drive home a new car for me every year. It was always the latest model, but the brand and color of his choosing. I once had to drive a red Cadillac with a red leather interior for two years even though I hate red and I don't like Cadillacs.

Was that an expensive gift? You bet! Was it a thoughtful one? Definitely not. I would have been a lot happier had I been involved in the selection process, or at least consulted, even if it had been a way less expensive car.

And now I'm gonna share with you guys a very special secret. Women, unlike men, don't like to be given practical gifts. Those they can go out and get themselves. I know a man who gave his girlfriend a tool box for Valentine's Day and then couldn't understand why the ungrateful thing threw him out of the house together with the box, red ribbon and all.

On the other hand, you don't have to spend a fortune to make a woman happy. Sometimes little things can do the trick if they are given with thoughtfulness and a special touch.

There is something that never fails to bring a smile to a woman's face. And that is flowers. Nothing spells out "you are special to me"--other than giving her diamonds, which is a whole different ball game--better than a bunch of beautiful flowers.

The freshness, the smell and the colors of a flower are equated in a woman's mind with everything that is soft and feminine. And the very fact that you spend your time and money on something as ephemeral and totally unnecessary as a flower just to say "I care" gets to the very soul of a woman.

Women Need to be Touched

Whoever coined the word "touchy-feely" must have been a woman. Nothing conveys feelings more directly than the sense of touch. And women are tuned into touching in a primal way. After all, what could be softer and more inviting than a baby's skin?

We hold, cuddle and smell babies very much like all primates do. Touching gives both us and the baby a sense of comfort. The female will always maintain that primal need to be touched. Perhaps what comes closest is the feel of a soft fabric against her skin. That's why silk and cashmere are such hits with women.

But even diamonds pale in comparison to the caress of a lover that is close to the heart. Dazzle her with diamonds, but please don't hold the caresses. Nothing feels better than the feel of your warm skin next to hers. Hold her hand when you cross the street. Few things make a woman feel more unprotected than to confront a possibly dangerous situation alone, even if it's just heavy traffic, particularly if her man is with her.

You see, it's more symbolic than real. She's a big girl now, and perfectly capable of crossing the street by herself. After all, she does it all the time when she's not with you. But to know you are there, steering her clear of trouble makes you look like her knight in shining armor. And it's no skin off your nose, so please hold her hand.

A Certain Kind of Touch

While we are on the subject of touch and hand holding, it's important to emphasize that your touch should be firm. No wishy-washy hand holding, please. A strong, firm touch conveys authority, a hesitant one denotes weakness. *And that's a real turn off.*

Remember when you went to your first social and asked your first girl for a dance? And how your hand trembled while you held her? No wonder the poor thing scurried back to her corner once the music stopped. Your hand felt well, *icky* on her back. Not to mention the sweat on your palm. But you're not fifteen any more-and neither is she. Hopefully she has had many more encounters with the opposite sex, and so have you, and if she is of a sensual nature, which for your sake I hope she is, she will welcome the warm, strong touch of a real man.

Only a Strong Man Can Afford to be Gentle

Gentleness, that quality that allows a man to treat a woman with a certain deference that makes her feel completely female, can only come from a strong man.

If this feels like a paradox, think again. A weak man may feel threatened by a strong woman. His reaction then is to try to dominate and subdue her, in order to feel superior. A strong man, on the other hand, can afford the luxury of letting a woman remain in her own level and still be able to deal with her comfortably, for he is coming from a place of strength.

Behind him are the testimony of countless encounters where he has come out a victor on his own turf. He has the self esteem that says: I can deal with my equal. He can listen and validate her opinions without losing ground, for he is in a lofty level himself.

Never confuse gentleness with weakness. A wise woman will be able to sort out the two. And, I ask of you, do you want any other kind? By now your woman probably knows that shouting and a show of force many times are a cover up, an armor used by a less than formidable opponent.

Should you Spoil Her?

First let's define what spoiling means.

In my book a man is to delight, flatter and made to feel absolutely wonderful. Whether that means cooking his favorite meal, wearing his favorite perfume, taking pains to look smashing for him. Not only on special occasions, but every single day. Doing what he asks of me when he asks it to the best of my ability and charming him with stories and witty conversation.

If a man is not making me feel like doing all these things, then he is not inspiring the passion that is in me. I believe that we all have the capacity to be passionate. All it takes is the right mix to create a combustion to ignite the flame.

On the other hand, I believe that I should inspire my man to do the same thing for me. Whether it is buying me a perfect rose on the spur of the moment, or surprising me with a pair of tickets to my favorite show, giving has to come from the heart, and it is nothing but the active translation of a feeling that started perhaps a week, a day or a month before.

Nobody should give out of guilt or a sense of duty. When that happens the results are always stilted. You notice it in the token you get, which usually falls short of what you want, or the giving comes with an afterthought that spoils the whole effect.

But when the giving is genuine, when it comes from a sense of wanting to please that special person about whom you have been thinking all day there is no danger of spoiling the recipient, for the gift will be seen as a physical manifestation of love, which is what giving really is.

Is there any danger of giving too much? Only if you are giving to the wrong person or you give too soon. If you wait until your love is ripe and deep, giving will only add points to your relationship.

Be a Good Escort

Few things can rattle more a woman than to take her beau to a party and see him disappear in front of the hors d'ouvre table or make a bee line for the bar.

You are there to escort her. To be at her side, get her drinks, engage her friends in conversation. In short, help her navigate a sometimes intimidating social situation. I'm not saying that you have to be glued to her, but be available for dancing, drink-getting and small talk. And don't even think of flirting with the redhead in the corner, even if she keeps looking your way. If you're really interested you'll run into her again. That type is always a return engagement at parties around town.

Be a Sport

I'm not telling you to spring for the check every time you go out with friends, but treating once in a while delights a woman. To see her man as a generous, gracious host endears him to her woman to no end. It spells out class and generosity, not only of the pocket, but also of the spirit.

I truly believe that human beings are divided into two categories: the accountants and the poets. The first ones are forever trying to figure out what they put into the world and what the world owes them. Whether it's love, respect or a free meal, they are busy reconciling their personal balance sheet, making sure the input--God forbid, never exceed the output, least some cataclysmic consequence ensues.

Then there are the poets. These gentle souls are lucky enough to figure out early on the nature of our higher purpose which, between you and me, even though volumes have been written about, and philosophers make a living out of trying to decipher it, I'm convinced is nothing more than to *enjoy*. Have I told you this before?

So you give a little more than you take in. Know what? You may enjoy the giving. So you love a little more than you are loved. If the truth be said, the lover is always happier than the beloved. All than intensity of feeling, the mere fact of being moved by another human being is sheer joy. I'd much rather participate in the entertainment than being enter-tained. Give me the active role over the passive. It's simply more fun.

If you need to choose, please be a poet--but also, every once in a while, show her you can be a sport!

www.ingramcontent.com/pod-product-compliance
Lightning Source LLC
LaVergne TN
LVHW091219080426
835509LV00009B/1077